FLOW

FLOW

Whanganui River Poems

Airini Beautrais

Victoria University Press

VICTORIA UNIVERSITY PRESS
Victoria University of Wellington
PO Box 600 Wellington
vup.victoria.ac.nz

Copyright © Airini Beautrais
First published 2017

This book is copyright. Apart from
any fair dealing for the purpose of private study,
research, criticism or review, as permitted under the
Copyright Act, no part may be reproduced by any
process without the permission of
the publishers

ISBN 9781776561148

A catalogue record is available at the National Library of New Zealand.

Published with the assistance of a grant from

Printed in China by 1010 Printing Group

He pākenga wai, he nohoanga tāngata
he nohoanga tāngata, he putanga kōrero

Where there is a body of water, people settle
and where people settle, legends unfold

Whanganui River proverb

Contents

Dedication   13

I. CATCHMENT

Map of Whanganui River Catchment   19

Confluence   21
Taumarunui, 2013

Plotlines   23
Waimarino, 2013

Clear away   25
Ōrākau, 1864

Hat on a map   27
Te Rohe Pōtae, 1870s

Pigs, potatoes   28
Te Kumi, 1883

A living sea   30
Te Nehenehenui, 1884

First sod of the Main Trunk Line   33
Pūniu, 1885

Surveyor's grave   34
Tāngarākau, 1893

Into the ground   35
Kākahi, 1905

Sound the whistle   36
Manunui, 1907

Inroads   37
Ōhura, 1913

Roads   38
Central Volcanic Plateau, 2013

Tree-oh! *Kākahi, 1914*	41
Only dancing *Kākahi, 1916*	43
That winter *Ōngarue, 1923*	45
The road out of here *Upper Retaruke, 1927*	46
Falling branch *Manunui, 1928*	48
Out of the ground *Waimiha, 1930s*	49
Three days *Horokino, 1936*	50
Up to their necks *Tokirima, 1940*	51
Eggs for an army *Ōngarue, 1940s*	52
Forgotten world *State Highway 43, 2014*	53
What sport to-night? *Ōngarue, 1953*	56
Cutting down King Mahuta *Ōngarue, 1950s*	57
Bush tram *Ōngarue, 1955*	58
Parts shed *Pureora, 1950s*	59
This'll do me *Ōngarue, 1962*	60

Oil drill   62
Ōtunui, 1966

Final whistle   63
Ōngarue, 1966

Treetops   64
Pureora, 1978

Buried forest   66
Pureora, 1983

Tributaries   67
Taumarunui to Piropiro, 2014

Huihui   69
Taumarunui, 2014

II. A BODY OF WATER

Map of Whanganui River	75
Puanga	77
Snow	80
Seed	82
Flow	84
Kākahi	85
Western diversion	86
Whio	87
Map-making	88
Shingle beach	90
Trout	91
Grayling	95
Spring—black, red and white	96
Kōura	99
Whirlpool	100
Dynamite	101
Fire	102

Hīnaki	108
Tuna	109
Foundlings	110
Lamprey	113
Moutoa	114
Summer	115
Girl with baby in a cornfield	118
Pandora's Box	119
Kauarapaoa	120
Children in the mud	122
Wattlebirds	124
Pākaitore	125
Flood	126
Girl with oranges	130
Spoonbill	132
Listen	133
Autumn	135

III. THE MOVING SAND

Map of Whanganui town	143
Geology	145
The long wait	146
Surprise	147
Beachcombing along the tidal reaches	148
Lieutenant	149
Open Country	150
Constable	151
Eunice	152
PechaKucha	153
Mrs Field	154
Shifting sand	155

The jail house	156
Holiday Park	157
Stormbird	158
Bluffs	159
Heads Road	160
Blood and sand	161
Gathering the berries of *Pimelea turakina*	162
Meat workers	163
Port Bowen	164
Glow in the dark	165
Longshore drift	166
The sandhill	167
Observatory	168
Dead port	169
Cyrena	170
Control	171
Walking the dog	172
The long wait II	173
South Beach Café	174
Grace Dent	175
Pour	176
North Mole	177
Selected bibliography	179
Acknowledgements	181

Dedication

In March 2017, the Te Awa Tupua Bill came into effect in New Zealand law. It follows on from the deed of settlement, Ruruku Whakatupua—*Te Mana o te Iwi o Whanganui*, signed by Whanganui iwi and the Crown in 2014. As well as a formal apology on behalf of the Crown and financial redress, the settlement takes the world-leading step of according legal personhood to the Whanganui River.

In 2012, when I was planning to write a series of poetic sequences about histories from the Whanganui region, there was increasing media attention to the planned granting of personhood status to the river. Initially I set out to write about quite disparate stories, the river being one focus among several. But water has a way of infiltrating things. A map of the Whanganui and its tributaries shows a thin line beginning on the slopes of Tongariro, heading north, bending at Taumarunui and heading southwest to the coast, widening as it goes. Along the way it draws in other lines: the main tributaries Ōngarue, Ōhura, Whakapapa, Tangarakau, Retaruke, Manganui-a-te-ao and all of the streams feeding into them, as well as many smaller streams, draining a total catchment area of over 7000 square kilometres. Te Awa Tupua views the river, tributaries and estuary as an integrated, indivisible living whole. As I wrote, the river drew in all the smaller stories to become the main focus of the work.

Writing about, or, more accurately, around the river, was not a straightforward task. As the work evolved into a single entity with the river as a focus, it also became less narrative. For one thing, it is impossible to tell 'the story' of a geographical region and its people: there are many stories relating to this place, and many interpretations of these stories. And, more importantly, the significance of the relationships between Whanganui iwi and the river cannot be adequately addressed by a Pākehā writer. Although six generations of my family have lived in this region on and off, and although I have a strong personal connection to the river, I felt that a unified narrative was beyond my understanding and capability, and that a fragmented approach was better suited to the way I wanted to respond to local geography and history. Another reason for avoidance of continuous narrative is time-scale. I've included poems set in geological time, through various stages of human settlement to the present. The nineteenth century is a particular focus, as is the current situation regarding climate change and environmental degradation.

This work is therefore not an attempt at a history of the river or its people. Rather, it is an attempt at something like a collage or polyphony of stories: some small, some large, some geological, some ecological, most human. The proverb used as an epigraph to this collection reminds us that stories collect around bodies of water because people live there. In all writing about landscape, human relationships with the landscape and with one another provide the greatest interest.

Another proverb that many people who know Whanganui will be familiar with is:

E rere kau mai te awa nui nei
Mai i te kāhui maunga ki Tangaroa
Ko au te awa
Ko te awa ko au

The great river flows
from the mountains to the sea
I am the river
and the river is me

In citing this proverb I would like to acknowledge the tangata whenua of Whanganui and the wider river region, whose lands this work is set in and whose stories are referenced. I would also like to acknowledge tau iwi and their various relationships to land, and their stories included here. A broad work calls for a broad dedication, so I would like to dedicate *Flow: Whanganui River Poems* to all the people of the river.

—Airini Beautrais, 2017

I. CATCHMENT

Well may these plundered and insulted kings,
Stripped of their robes, despoiled, uncloaked, discrowned
Draw down the clouds with white enfolding wings

—William Pember Reeves, 'The Passing of the Forest'

Did you hear the Bush a-calling, when your heart was young and bold
'I'm the Mother-Bush that nursed you! Come to me when you are old?'

—Henry Lawson, 'On the Night Train'

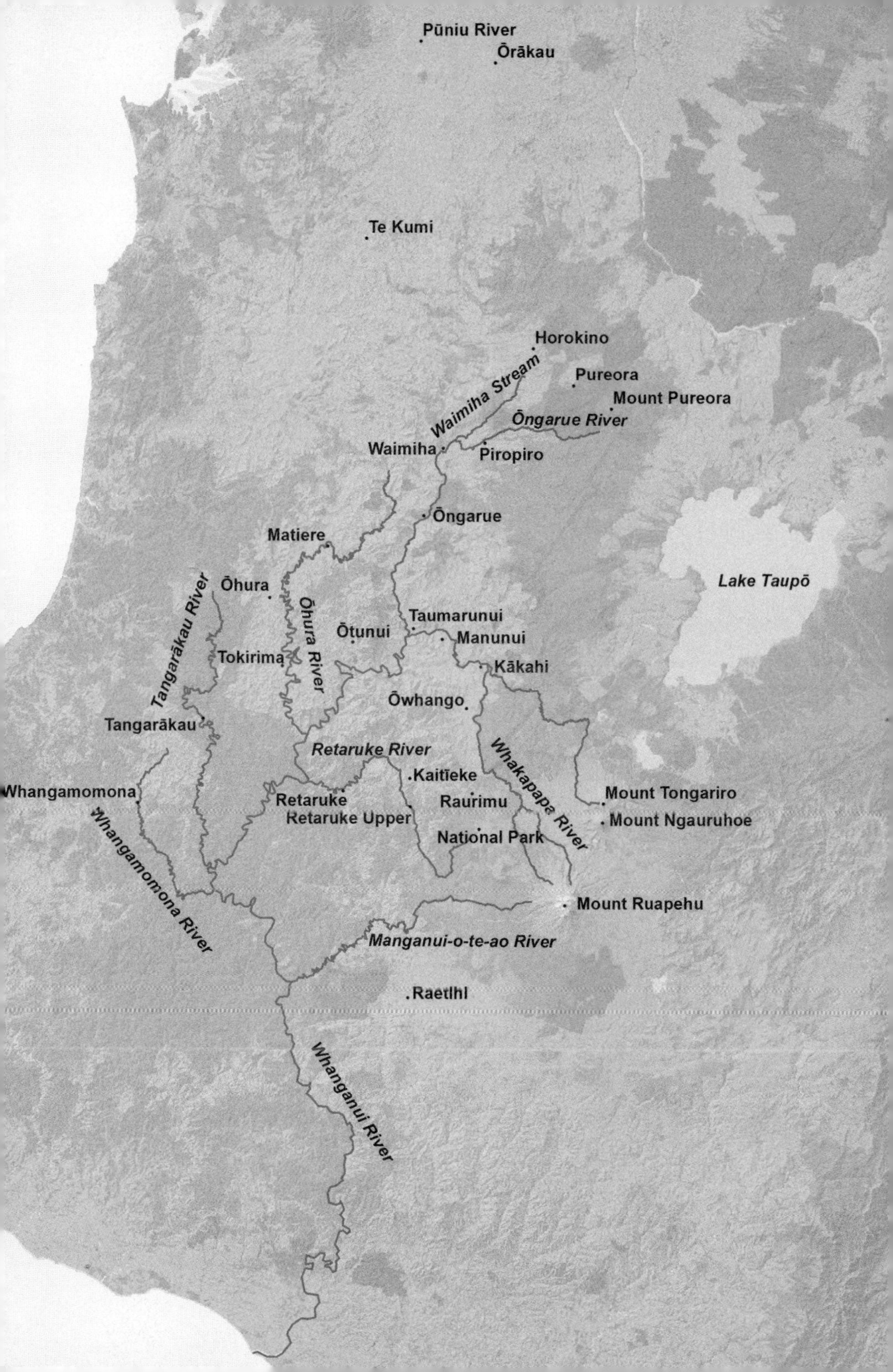

Pūniu River
Ōrākau
Te Kumi
Horokino
Waimiha Stream
Pureora
Mount Pureora
Ōngarue River
Waimiha
Piropiro
Ōngarue
Matiere
Lake Taupō
Ōhura
Tangarākau River
Ōhura River
Taumarunui
Ōtunui
Manunui
Tokirima
Kākahi
Ōwhango
Tangarākau
Retaruke River
Whakapapa River
Kaitīeke
Whangamomona
Mount Tongariro
Retaruke
Raurimu
Retaruke Upper
Mount Ngauruhoe
National Park
Whangamomona River
Mount Ruapehu
Manganui-o-te-ao River
Raetihi
Whanganui River

Confluence
Taumarunui, 2013

Two rivers meet, at an acute angle,
hold a point of ground in their fork.
Although this place is called Cherry Grove,
there are only a few cherries,

and not the edible type. Looking down Whanganui,
one bank grows willows and Japanese walnuts;
the other, corn and half a tōtara, unbranched
by the wind. It's the end of a dry summer:

wine connoisseurs have been rubbing
hands together, anyone with grass
has been downcast. Ōngarue is clean-looking;
deep, dark brown of tannins, slight scent of algae,

thistledown drifting on its surface.
'Most rivers are clean this time of year,' says Joe,
my brother, 'because the only water going in them
is ground water; there's no run-off.'

Standing at the confluence,
you can see the join in the rivers; either side
a different colour and speed.
Like standing at Cape Reinga watching two oceans

seam together.
'The Whangaehu, though,' says Joe,
'the Whangaehu is *never* clean. I don't know why.' We sit
on the spit, watch Joe flick his line, the rod bend

almost immediately. It's a big one, and must be played.
Joe tells the line and the line tells the fish, leap there,
and it's ashore. Joe's netless since he dropped it
in the Mohaka, has taken to braining trout with a rock,

rather than knifing between the eyes, like he taught me.
People will do all kinds of things to come down to earth.
The trout have been eating caddis-fly pupae, algae, stones.
'I found a dragonfly in one once,' Joe says. 'It was still alive.'

Joe's misplaced the tray from the smoker,
so he builds one of willow, and we eat the trout
a few metres from where he caught it,
with bread, and wild greens harvested from New World.

I walk the baby to sleep along the bank,
among the disposable nappies, circles of bourbon bottles.
Tea from a thermos, talk of our grandparents.
I've bought Joe a kilo of frozen peas, to take a fish north.

'You know how people say, Oh, the good old days,'
Joe says. 'I think I'll remember these as the good old days.'
We leave him there, parked up. He'll sleep in the car,
drift off to the sound of water, the poplar leaves slapping.

Plotlines
Waimarino, 2013

Driving into Raetihi, you're greeted by the graveyard.
The town is on side-roads, the main street has a frontier look,
with the kind of useless false-fronts Laura Ingalls hated
in *Little Town on the Prairie*. Though it's not tumbleweeds

blowing down this street, but mountain air, and a clarity
that comes with coldness, a light distilled.
Buildings on the point of collapse, an empty theatre.
I imagine Friday night in the fifties, feet sounding

in and out of doors, plotlines of the real unfolding
in the back seats, or down the road a way.
In the charity shop, an impromptu coffee group is underway.
I look through racks of ripped jackets, holed pants.

'I stuffed up my interview. They asked me
"What are the three Ps of the Treaty of Waitangi?"
And I said Um . . . People . . .'
I am tempted to join in their conversation,

but get a sense it's better if I'm barely here.
'Most people wouldn't know that. I don't even know that. What
                                        are the three Ps?'
'Partnership, participation, protection.'
Or maybe it's the sense that I *shouldn't* be here,

that I have accidentally stumbled into the set
of someone's life, not even an extra in the script.
'They asked me that in my interview too, and I didn't know.
So I just said People, peace, and . . . pineapples!'

I keep sifting, nothing's leaping out. Good books can hide
among the shirtless rugby players of years gone by.
You can't argue with the view from here.
I've never seen Ruapehu looking so bare.

According to the National Institute
for Water and Atmospheric Research, we can expect,
by the year 2099, a 2.2 degree average increase in temperature,
shortened duration of seasonal snow, rise in snowline . . .

My son always wants a story. Tell me a story about a T-rex
who was far away. Tell me a story about a spider
who was lonely. And if the plotline doesn't develop:
'That wasn't a story! I want a proper story!'

Obstacle, obstacle, obstacle, solution.
Even a three-year-old knows the basic devices.
Obstacle, obstacle, obstacle, attempted solution, failure.
The greatest stories of all time are geological.

Clear away
Ōrākau, 1864

Orchard:
They carved their bullets from my wood,
the peach too soft to be much good,
but apple, solid, worked all right.
No use in wasting lead at night.

Field:
The soldiers dug their ugly sap,
then swarmed into its earthen gap.
The cannons groaned, the fuses took,
With every booming shell, I shook.

Fence:
The soldier's body was still warm.
Blood ran from where his uniform
was torn. The chief passed, while he bled.
'Do not cut out his heart,' he said.

Hill:
No water left, their throats were dry,
food hard to swallow. 'We will die,'
warned Rewi, 'if we wait a day.'
They shouldered axes, guns. They'd stay.

Palisade:
Surrounded, Rewi ordered: 'Fire!'
Major Mair brought word: 'Ceasefire.
Surrender now.' The answer: 'Never.
My friend, we'll fight forever and ever.'

Fern:
But time came to retreat. As one,
they broke their cover, were fired upon.
Some of the wounded, women. They
were bayoneted where they lay.

Pūniu River:
The living swam, and found a track.
The Pākehā were falling back.
South of here, they journeyed on.
Clear away. Then they were gone.

Hat on a map
Te Rohe Pōtae, 1870s

One million acres gone,
Waikato journey in.
Across the river's boundary,
Maniapoto country.

Down here, the trees hold sway.
No wide and cloudless sky,
no gentle rolling dales,
these gorges and these hills.

Tāwhiao's white bell-topper
lands on the map's wide paper.
The border of its brim
holds each range and stream.

No Pākehā. No surveys.
No land court, and no railways.
No liquor, and no Crown.
The rivers spine on spine.

Somewhere, Te Kooti shelters
from the colonial soldiers.
The countless pathways mingle
in this wet and silent jungle.

Pigs, potatoes
Te Kumi, 1883

They name two pigs for us, to kill, and cook,
and feast upon. We hear them chant outside
the small slab hut where we are kept, hands tied
by manacle and chain. 'No one will look

for us out here,' sighs Newsham. And he's right,
how many miles we are from any track.
I feel a knot of bruise upon my back,
where I was struck by stirrup iron that night,

two days ago, or one? It's hard to tell.
In cold and smoke I feel my bare skin shrink.
Our bowl of water isn't fit to drink,
being soured with blood. That maddening smell:

our porcine namesakes roasting on the fire.
They've thrown us pigs' potatoes, green and raw,
but they've rolled from our reach. The earthen floor
is hard beneath my bones as I retire,

attempting sleep. The chiefs have been talked round,
but it would seem not everyone's disposed
towards this railway. And so the survey's nosed
a little further, only to be found

out by Tekau-mā-rua. Now here we are.
'My pipe was in my coat,' my cellmate cries,
hands jerking uselessly. They must despise
me most of all, since that time at the pā

at Parihaka, where I was the one
who placed the survey pegs, which they removed.
I work at freeing a hand. By day, it's proved
successful. Then the light reveals a gun

poked round the door. A man walks in.
'It is I, it is I, my children,' comes his voice.
It is Te Kooti. All of us rejoice.
I greet him choked with tears as thick as sin.

A living sea
Te Nehenehenui, 1884

Up at Te Kumi there's a gallows built
to hang the Native Minister, if he
should venture there. But I have travelled lands
of ill repute before, and have no fear.

My sole intention being to advance
the scientific interests of this land,
I'll not let any obstacle impede
my course, save force. 'If you should meet . . .

with Mahuki,' we're told, 'you may be chained
like Hursthouse was, or get a bullet through
your head.' We leave the pack horse and my gun.
Te Wheu takes us to where the forest starts.

With so much open country hitherto,
the leafy scenery seems a welcome change.
But pathless woods can lose their pleasure fast:
dark trunks, sly vines that coil round neck and feet.

The ground as slippery as if it were glass,
our two remaining horses crouch and slide.
The muddy creeks so terrify the beasts
we have to flog them over, every time.

They leap on fallen trees, jump down like dogs.
And now we notice we are bearing down
into the valley of the Whanganui.
The night comes fast, we make camp in a swamp.

The ground so rooted-up it seems to me
to be some kind of pig-Elysium.
We make our beds of nīkau fronds. The rain
pours down from branches, slicks around our necks.

Leaving this 'Dismal Swamp' at dawn, we pray
we never come upon this place again.
Not long into our walk the forest breaks,
a valley parts, a bright clear river strung

through it—the Manganui-o-te-ao.
We hear a voice shout *Pākehā!* Then out
from hiding, people circle us. They send
a messenger to fetch their chief, who comes

gun shouldered, hand in easy trigger's reach.
'What brings you through the forest?' we are asked.
'We're travelling for pleasure,' we explain.
And all burst into laughter, even the dogs.

'Their horses look like rats,' an old man cries.
'These Pākehā,' he adds, 'have singular ways.'
But then the oldest woman rises up
and calls us in with eerie wailing sounds.

Her words appear to have a magic charm:
the horses watered, feasting is prepared.
Potatoes, apples, pork rendered in fat.
My stomach curls with hunger at the smell.

The morning comes. Our journey far from over,
we pack our gear, farewell our new-found friends.
'If Manganui don't land you here again,'
the chief says, 'you may have to eat your nags.'

First sod of the Main Trunk Line
Pūniu, 1885

There was a boy who shook and shook his hat,
but I stood still, no matter how the heat
annoyed me, how the lace cut at my throat,
how my head hurt. Giving my back a pat,

my father looked away into the green.
There were these painted men, each with a crown
of feathers, on the barrow. Dark red skin.
They didn't look like any men I'd seen.

It seemed like hours and hours and hours I stood.
My father spoke, as plainly as he could.
Then the Premier did, and the crowd
all cheered as Wahanui cut the sod.

Surveyor's grave
Tāngarākau, 1893

A road to map, we worked the chain
Lay me down, lay me down
We worked in sun, we worked in rain
Oh lay me down on the moss.

But deep, far deep, in dip and hill
Lay me down, lay me down
While we were camping, I took ill
Oh lay me down on the moss.

My belly tight with stabbing pain
Lay me down, lay me down
I'll never know my home again
Oh lay me down on the moss.

Send for the doctor, walk the track
Lay me down, lay me down
But I'll be done before you're back
Oh lay me down on the moss.

See that the farm goes to my wife
Lay me down, lay me down
And wish my child a prosperous life
Oh lay me down on the moss.

Into the ground
Kākahi, 1905

Our 'hotel' is a canvas tent, and every brew we sell
is made from—if you'd like a glass, it's best if I don't tell.
What we don't know won't kill us, the navvies usually say.
They turn up in a crowd at dusk, to drink the night away.

And when they've spent their pay on booze, and danced with me
                                                and Jane,
there's nothing left for them to do but start a fight again.
The reverends are at home in bed, beside their rigid wives.
The Holy City has the coppers fearing for their lives.

I'm with a fellow lying in the shadow of the wall
when by the bar a scuffle forms, and swells into a brawl.
A lantern is knocked over, then a flagon of potcheen
and soon the flames are licking all around the whole shebeen.

Jane shrieks like there's a knife in her, the man beside me stands
and offers his assistance, holding out his leathery hands.
But I'm a faster runner. I know how to work that floor.
I claw my way past drunken men and sprint out through the door.

I look back over my shoulder, and the whole town is alight,
bright orange like a ship's flare in the black and silent night.
I see women in their nightgowns, their hair all loose and wild,
under one arm a bundle, and the other a screaming child.

We shelter in the railway cuttings, safe within the stone.
Jane cries into my mantle, but I've no tears of my own.
The Holy City's up in smoke. I shudder at the sound,
but mostly I am pleased to see it go into the ground.

Sound the whistle
Manunui, 1907

Down the tight line the lokey shakes and veers
its train of logs. The nervous brakey peers
around the gap. We'll be the first across
Burnand's new bridge. I've worked here, now, two years

as driver, like to think I'll never leave.
Though it's no Auckland, I've come to believe
it's home. The load smells damp, the wet tracks glow,
sun flashes in the bridge's diamond weave;

and entering it, I let the whistle crow.
A scream so loud it's like the sound could go
halfway around the world. And then we meet
the other bank, the smokestack's steady flow;

the whine of saws comes tearing through the heat
of early afternoon. This is our feat:
the first logs over the Punga. Manunui!
We swing into the yards on Totara Street.

Inroads
Ōhura, 1913

Sunrise lights the valley's pipe,
spits polish on the camera lens.
I pack my notebook and my pens,
and give my muddy shoes a wipe.

A pointless task. The horses climb,
the buggy teeters, overfull,
its wheels sink deeper every pull.
We could have walked in half the time.

A farmer whistles to his dogs,
a tide of sheep weaves through the stumps.
The roadworkers are laying lumps
of greyish clay on piles of logs

and stuffing smaller logs between.
'It's papa rock. We bake it there,
for metalling roads. No shingle here.'
'The strangest thing I've ever seen,'

I say. I think of Homer, how
he told the way a funeral pyre
was built. The kindling catches fire,
the logs flare up, then char, then glow

the while we stand there, looking on.
'Well, I suppose you have a lot
of wood round here.' But there is not
a grove left standing—all is gone.

Roads
Central Volcanic Plateau, 2013

At National Park, the railway station café
is playing nu-jazz, selling Wellingtonesque food.
No ladies' rest, no tearooms. Time-travel
is becoming increasingly difficult. Where

is my indestructible teacup? Where is my pink lamington?
We eat lunch at Whakapapa Village,
rain gushing all over the mountain.
Sit in a public shelter, strewn with possum scat.

No tables to coax the kids to. They crawl and run.
A happy-looking couple walk through to the toilets;
thumping ensues. Some kind of a bet, I guess.
Leave your down jacket on, hon; it's freezing here.

They climb back in their car as quickly as they came.
In the info centre I feel for the teacher
instructing with questions, getting grunts
for answers. My sons try to muscle their way

through the forest of legs to the table
with a plaster model of the mountains,
buttons that make little red lights glow.
Volcanoes! Volcanoes! From the Age of the Dinosaurs!

Displays must be examined, then climbed.
The AV feature tells stories it has told for years,
which, it has recently emerged, aren't entirely factual.
The word 'gift' something of a misnomer

given some of the land in the park was taken.
There was an occupation at Taurewa, a few years back;
a couple of caravans, and waving flags, but the tussocklands
as we pass them now, are empty of all but tussocks.

I want to find the Whanganui intake, but drive in squares
through blocks of licheny pines. I find, instead, a hump of grass
like a wave about to break over the car, and climb it
to see sodden fishermen in oilskins, dipping lines in a lake.

The rain stops just before Turangi. Under the bridge
at dusk, we find more anglers to watch.
Lukas fishes with a twig, catches willow leaves.
All along the river, the pools are staked out, lines flicker.

In the morning, Highway 41, over the Punga.
This road was built, in part, by Rene Beautrais
II and III (Beautrais and Son). In Taumarunui
we walk every row of the old cemetery,

looking for Rene Beautrais I, and Elizabeth.
How we link to France, and Ireland.
Wet leaves lie everywhere, fly-agarics bloom.
'Fliegenpils! Fliegenpils!' chants Lukas, fan of fungi.

I find the grave, scratch lichen from the headstone.
It stains my fingernails, dark brown.
It was a fiery family. And anyone
who might have been inclined to tend

these cracking slabs is dead.
If I come here again, I'll bring a brush,
and clean it properly,
at least so the names can be read.

Tree-oh!
Kākahi, 1914

The whistle-boy pulls on the line,
lets out a rush of steam.
Stoke the hauler full of wood
and hear that piping scream.
Tree-oh!
Hear that piping scream.

The swing of arms into the axe,
the crosscut's symmetry.
The sound of thunder in the ground
when bushmen drop a tree.
Tree-oh!
The bushmen drop the tree.

The strain is great, the hauler groans,
the rope-man walks the bush.
Uneven ground before a log,
it takes charge with a rush!
Tree-oh!
It takes charge with a rush.

The brakey works his wooden blocks
The train shakes down the tracks.
Hack a hold into a log
and hold on to your axe!
Tree-oh!
Hold on to your axe.

The trucks are brought down to the mill
two hundred feet below.
A smoking of the wooden brakes,
she moves in nice and slow.
Tree-oh!
She moves in nice and slow.

The log is sawn, the lunch bell's gone,
go home and raise your cup.
While sitting at the giant teeth
saw doctor sharpens up.
Tree-oh!
Saw doctor sharpens up.

Mill No. 2 is all cut out,
two years for No. 1.
There'll be a strange peace settles here
with all the bushmen gone.
Tree-oh!
With all the bushmen gone.

Only dancing
Kākahi, 1916

I wish you'd found me Tuesday night
down at the station, Dave.
I could have faced you man to man
and heard you rant and rave.

Instead you stayed at home three days,
the devil in your head.
You made your hut a pit of death,
a bath of blood your bed.

They say that Bulltown got its name
from wild beasts clashing there.
If we had fought it out like that—
I'm sorry Dave, I swear.

Sure, there were rumours going round
I'd got myself in strife.
There may have been a grain of truth—
but nothing with your wife.

Sure, she's a lovely lady,
the best dancer of them all.
How smooth her dress beneath my hand
at the Military Ball.

But dancing—that was all it was!
It always made you sore.
'I'm leaving town,' I said to her,
'come twirl with me once more.'

You knew the way the talk had turned,
the rancor and the rot.
You said she mustn't look at me;
she didn't see why not.

You'd stayed at home, you weren't to see,
but gossip spreads like flu,
and twisted tales soon found their way
around the town to you.

Pea-rifle pressed against her head,
you fired. Then, one by one,
you went to each of your six kids
and beat them with the gun.

What words could I have said to you?
What words had turned your brain?
You're with your children in the ground;
we'll never speak again.

The mill closed down not long ago,
you'd joined a roading crew.
To read it like this in the *Truth*—
and how they've mangled you!

My music was your music, mate:
the saws, the axe's thud.
I'll never be back to Bulltown now
come fire or come flood.

That winter
Ōngarue, 1923

That winter, light went sooner from the hill.
I walked my boundary fence same way I had
for twenty years, and watched the boulders spill
onto the line. This spot was always bad;

I'd told them time and time again to make
a deviation, take my corner field.
But every time, deaf ears. What was at stake
was more than I would risk. Something would yield,

these weeks and weeks of rain. And then it did—
one icy morning, keeping to the clock,
the Auckland–Wellington express train slid
around the bend, and met the latest rock.

The feeble headlight no match for the night,
the gas-line carbide blocked, the engine hit
before the brakes were touched. The ugly light
of dawn lit up the wreckage, sleepers split

to kindling, rails ripped up, the boiler smashed.
Two carriages had telescoped to one,
and on the back of that, a third had crashed.
The living staunchly did what could be done.

Inquiry found the railways not to blame,
they couldn't have foreseen it. Strike me dumb!
Whatever they said, the dead remained the same.
I grasped my black umbrella, and kept mum.

The road out of here
Upper Retaruke, 1927

My granddad Hursthouse told these tales, the wildest I had heard
of being tied up, and almost cooked. I hung on every word.
When I came back from fighting in the war with Germany
what other place but King Country?
The King Country for me!

I got five hundred acres with a soldier's rehab loan.
Till my heart strained, I worked the land I hoped I'd someday own.
I chopped the bush, then came the slump to smack me in the eye.
I watched the wool price plummeting
I watched my prospects die.

I needed land. I made a deal: I'll chop, you buy the seed.
The government man was willing and he readily agreed.
But when I'd done, the deal fell through—they wouldn't pay a cent.
I'd rather deal with Lucifer
than with the government.

So I set to and burned the bush, burned all the valleys bare.
They'll have to sow it now, I thought, they'll have to make it square.
How wrong I was, left broke and sick, no fodder for my sheep.
How do they get away with it?
How do those scoundrels sleep?

The Commissioner for Farmers came, could not believe his eyes.
That soldier-settlers have been had, a fool could realise.
He said the land was mine for free, but didn't twist my arm.
I can't take one more week of this
I can't take any farm.

A glance around the second growth, you'd never know a man
had wasted five years here. Well, now I'm doing the last I can:
a few clothes and a blanket roll, two ponies and their gear,
I'll walk the road down Retaruke,
the long road out of here.

Falling branch
Manunui, 1928

How strange the sky went sudden bright
when something struck me back of head.
Leaves sticking to my skull I lay
still as the dead.

Warm-handled axe still folded in
a ponga lying where it fell.
I'd knocked a heavy branch, as far
as I could tell.

They scooped their hands beneath my back,
they loaded me onto the train.
The sky kept going bright, then pale
then bright again.

The hospital so vast and bare
that every whisper seemed a shout.
I stared the brightness in the eye
till it went out.

Out of the ground
Waimiha, 1930s

They brought the bird in. My heart fairly sank.
Their father had been felling, and had found
it in the bush. 'We'll use the empty tank
by the back door.' He'd dragged it from the ground,

and under it were these two eggs. No chance
that they would hatch—the children's pets all died.
Dazed by the light, it did its wingless dance,
searched for a hole to roll its eggs inside.

Three days
Horokino, 1936

She sat there three days on the line.
Her cloak was soaking with the rain.
The tracks were wet, the earth was brown.
She blocked the line three days.

Down at the mill the work was slow,
because the loco couldn't go.
The boss fumed, but what could he do
away down at the mill?

They tried in vain to talk to her
but didn't dare to touch a hair,
and so she kept on sitting there;
kept silent as they tried.

They heard her say that they were cursed:
she cursed their bridges all to dust;
she hoped their tracks would bend and rust,
they heard her speak a curse.

And when she finally walked out
she said, 'Now here's another thought,
I'll see you fellows all in court.'
As slowly she walked out.

Up to their necks
Tokirima, 1940

The rising water's three feet deep
inside the church. The banks all seep;
the roadway is as thick as glue.
O Lord, have mercy on our crew.

The rivers tear apart the guts
of towns, rip bridges from their struts;
the streets are travelled by canoe.
O Lord, have mercy on our crew.

To every road the flood's unmade
they've sent us out. What good's a spade,
compared to what the rain can do?
O Lord, have mercy on our crew.

We've been inside this hut all day,
and now the ground is giving way—
we're buried if we don't get through.
O Lord, have mercy on our crew.

Eggs for an army
Ōngarue, 1940s

Lucky winter weather! The line is blocked up
with another slip, and the train is filled with
soldiers! Here we come in our dancing dresses,
rushing to greet them.

One by one, the houses light up like flowers,
doors thrown open. Usher them in, to sleep on
sofas, hearth rugs. And in the morning, all our
eggs in their pockets.

Forgotten world
State Highway 43, 2014

The Whangamomona hotel smells
like my grandma's house. Dust, grease,
newspapers. Rugby photos deck the walls,
men leaning in on shields. Hog's heads,

antlers, dry and spiderwebby. We drink tea,
eat toasted sandwiches. At the next table
an Australian family, kids almost grown.
'I just love these country pubs,' says the mother,

'they've got so much character.' A pub crawl drives up,
drunk at midday. Middle years,
in coloured wigs. To and from the bathroom.
'Someone's been shavin' 'er minge in the sink,'

bawls a man, delightedly. Kitted out
in their cute cardigans, my sons are set
to trash everything, bouncing off walls.
'I just love those hand-knitted clothes,'

says the Australian mum. She's going to make some
for a baby on the way.
Out in the sun, two farmers down a jug,
rurally handsome. A lurking dog

scares the kids. 'It's a friendly dog,'
I reassure them. 'You just missed
the friendly goat,' says a farmer,
pointing to where an animal's pissed,

right by his seat. 'It's not every day
you sit down for a beer and a goat pisses
next to you,' I laugh, but maybe, for them, it is.
That strange pang of wanting

to drink with locals, but we drive on.
Past Tāngarākau, 'Ghost Town'.
The hills look like they have undercuts,
the sides shorn close, trees left on top,

where it's too steep to fell. Roads unsealed,
dirty and skiddy. We reach Ōhura,
nestled in a circle of hills. Check in
at the former prison, chickens

and sheep wandering the grounds.
Any jailbreaker would have taken
a long time to escape to anywhere.
My mother's friends lived in the town a year.

'The only socialising was Tupperware parties,
and, as a teacher's wife, Sophie was expected
to spend up large.' At the museum
there's a lot of china. The Raurimu spiral

on a teacup. Long white christening gowns.
A stuffed ferret, a kiwi spitting larval droppings:
something has been eating it from within.
Rusty dental pliers, hardened saddles,

a slab hut brought in from the hills.
How did a family live there, five kids,
one tiny sackcloth bed? At the prison
we sleep in the old Programmes building.

Corrections signage everywhere,
shelves with staff mug spots still named.
Why is the most disturbing place
the kitchen? Rosters still chalked up:

who was on dishes,
who was on brush and shovel.
The lounge is stacked with books
kids must have leafed through, on visits.

Over and over, we read *Blueberries for Sal*.
When we go to look at the jail cells,
Felix thinks we might find blueberries there.
Or little bears.

What sport to-night?
Ōngarue, 1953

My borrowed lipstick has a stale fat scent.
We're the boys of the Ōngarue team
When we're on the field we look so grand
Black kohl and turquoise eye-shadow, that's good.

Kingdoms are clay. And that's the truth, round here:
the rugby clubroom always reeks of earth
and booted grass, and all the punters have
that smell, like they were cut just yesterday

by God from naked soil. I hear a call,
'Where's Cleopatty?' 'She's, or he's, out back,
having a fag.' I stub the butt, adjust
my padded bra. I could get used to this.

There's not a minute of our lives should stretch
without some pleasure now. Boys will be girls,
and that's Shakespearean, or so they say.
There's not a script, as such. We know a bit

by heart, but all the punters want is laughs.
I lie prone on the couch, gaze longingly
while Antony, with false nose, strokes his chin.
All through the hall, the women shriek, their jars

of coins keep filling, and the mugs flow over.
Most of our fortunes shall be—drunk to bed.
The rugby club could use a bob or two.
They laugh so hard they don't see how it ends.

Cutting down King Mahuta
Ōngarue, 1950s

The slap of hand on bark a kind of prayer.
The groan of heartwood as the rimu leans
and falls. 'King Mahuta,' boss says, to air.
We're quiet, know exactly what he means.

Bush tram
Ōngarue, 1955

Mary, Martha, Matilda—the locos all have
women's names, and even the 'Climax' warrants
'she'. The smell of tea-tree reminds me I am
dying to light up.

'Smokers please be careful,' the pamphlet tells us.
Bending over, all of the men are pointing
cameras. Now and then, they compare equipment,
peer in the workings.

How my husband turns to a boy, round steam trains!
'Absolutely *no souvenirs*,' I tell him.
'Hands in pockets, love, or you might be tempted.'
He doesn't listen.

'Monday,' says the driver, 'we start on lifting
all the track from here to the clearing.' Passing
through, we see the last of the branch line. Martha
ending her toiling.

Just to soothe a man, you will calmly travel
deep in darkest bushwhacker country, smiling
while he prattles. Climax, that loving woman
silently smoking.

Parts shed
Pureora, 1950s

The guy in charge of stores was a right prick
and so was I. We came down for a check
at Pureora. Took us a whole week.
I can't complain; I love that sort of work.

There was no end to all the things they had,
and they were beautiful, American-made,
from Caterpillar tracks right down to bits
of carburettor; all these fine new parts.

It was a working forest; native trees,
not like at Kaingaroa, those millions of pines.
There was no need for forestry degrees:
the work all done by powerful machines.

The whole thing was extremely powerful.
What the government had done was really good.
Me, I'm just happy dreaming of that shed
and all the parts I would have liked to steal.

This'll do me
Ōngarue, 1962

Keys are often kept in trouser pockets,
and this is where I find them, in the dark
cloth shape slung over a chair. In double bed
the postman and his wife breathe, out of time.

Their bedroom has a human smell, of sheets
and scalps. I'd rather rob an empty house—
you feel the silence welcome you, almost,
when first the window gives, then you ease in.

I always clean up afterwards, leave thanks
by way of note. Most of the year a bach
is shelter going to waste. The master's key,
hello, hello, fits nicely in the safe.

Three hundred pounds. Why thank you, now I'll go.
I tiptoe out, exhale into the night.
A short way down the road, a van is parked
outside the store—delivery, looks like.

This'll do me. The engine thrums, the road
rolls underneath. Like everything, it's fun,
just for a while. The days, or weeks, I'm out.
Time blurs. The roadblock takes me by surprise:

soldiers and cops. Their bullets whizz and ping
off panel and roof. I reckon I can run
faster than them, again. It's fit-and-lean
they drag me from the bush, back to the world

in back of Black Maria. Now there's spies
at large in Wellington, and music plays:
'Mister George Wilder, oh won't you come home.'
Oh, Howard Morrison, keep up your song.

Oil drill
Ōtunui, 1966

They're building rigs to drill for oil
the auger creeps down through the soil
and every kettle's on the boil
in Ōtunui, in Ōtunui.

We'll all be mighty stinking rich
when black gold gushes from that ditch
we feel our fingers start to twitch
in Ōtunui, in Ōtunui.

But—shit a brick, the rock is struck
it's typical of local luck
no boom has come, and we're still stuck
in Ōtunui, in Ōtunui.

Protestant popes and flying pigs
will come and dance around our digs
when oil is pouring from the rigs
in Ōtunui, in Ōtunui.

Final whistle
Ōngarue, 1966

Now it's happened, even the sound is startling
like a braking train, or a morepork hunting.
All of us are here in the bulging cookhouse,
laughing and eating.

When we started here, I was told the men would
need a bit of mothering. Sure, they did, but
it was like a family. Well, I don't know
why I am crying,

thinking of the bush and its eerie sadness,
rain collapsing all of the things we made here.
Still, I know they've sawn every dip and ridge, left
nothing of value.

Treetops
Pureora, 1978

I stood there, in the clearfell.
I heard the chainsaw's grinding speech
and over that, a kākā's screech.
At the same time, there came a swell

of song. It was a haunting sound,
as if the kōkako could weep
for all that came beneath the sweep
of dozers as they bared the ground.

I knew what we would have to do.
We gathered eighty friends or so,
and brought them down, so they would know
the threat first-hand. But no one knew

what we had planned. When they'd gone back,
we made our next move, went and got
a camping permit. There was not
one law being broken. Near the track,

but not too close, we chose our trees.
My brother made a whistling noise.
We'd climbed a lot of trees as boys,
but never ones as big as these.

First up, we threw a bit of string
to pull a rope, and then we tried
to climb the rātā vines. Inside
the canopy, we felt its swing,

we breathed its must, ancient and green.
The TV filmed us sitting there,
they had the District Ranger swear
on every household's telly screen,

'We've searched the bush—it's all a hoax.'
We'd simply hid too cleverly.
The Forest Service spoke to me
through media message, tried to coax

me down and out, but I stayed put,
possession being nine-tenths of law.
A fight was not what we came for.
But here's what hit them in the gut:

one day my brother, keeping still,
saw loggers come through, marking wood.
They scarfed the tree next door. He stood
his ground. A trunk's impact could kill,

depending on the way it dropped.
It hit the earth, and he was thrown
around. He made his presence known.
It shook them up. The logging stopped

soon after that. But it was plain
the fight went on—the hardest push
was working to restore the bush,
to stitch these fragments up again.

Buried forest
Pureora, 1983

And there it was. While trying to drain the swamp,
they hit the logs. 'It looks like they've been buried
a while,' we're told. Two thousand years, almost.
So bulldozing was paused, the book of time

looked into. What we found was really clear:
the soil this wood had grown on had been poor.
Over the trees the blasts of pumice fell,
and new bush grew, the type that loves rich soil.

And if the trees are left to do their thing,
the soil will slowly lose its wealth again.
Then, no doubt, that caldera will go off
and put another layer of bounty down.

Tributaries
Taumarunui to Piropiro, 2014

With a blunt stick my father cleans the lichen
from around his great grandparents' names.
It's grown back since last year.
My mother joins in, scraping moss from the slab.

On each side a long, thin cross. The fliegenpils
have popped up from the same mycorrhizal groove,
but Lukas is collecting acorns, stuffing them
in rear pockets. 'It will feel funny when you sit down,' I tell him.

Hazelnuts and Japanese walnuts
drop their fruit all around the graves. One hazel
springs up from where a young mother
was buried with her baby.

There's a Burnand monument, names wearing away,
rows of soldiers' crosses, and a neighbourhood of headstones,
days apart, for the 1918 flu epidemic. This cemetery
is as far back as we know our Beautrais whakapapa.

The road becomes Ōngarue Back Road,
becomes a dirt road, ends up in the quiet village.
On the grass verge a group of curly haired cyclists,
smiling and covered with mud.

'Trev used to come here a lot,' says my dad.
We follow the Ōngarue River, as it narrows
and grows cleaner, up Ōngarue Stream Road
through hills dark with untended pines.

At Piropiro campsite an apple tree, hung with lichen,
moss, and ripe apples. Is it a tree from the old days?
Is it a heritage variety? 'Tastes like a Gala to me,' says Dad.
At the forest's edge a group of Germans cook dinner.

Their voices carry in the still, cold air.
We walk the gravel track towards the Timber Trail.
Here and there various conifers are spotted,
remnants of the Forest Service experiments.

'They vindictively clearfelled, then replanted with pines,
Douglas Fir, or whatever they felt like,' says Dad.
'Whaddaya mean, *vindictively*?' asks my mum.
'Every time we said "Why don't we protect this bit?"

they went in and logged it.' 'Who sat up the trees?'
I ask them. 'Oh, Stephen, Bernard . . .'
'Sam . . .' The twilight
comes in, all soupy and violet. The forest

gives off its night perfume. We walk until dark.
It feels like the bush will swallow us up.
A robin follows us out, hiding in the mānuka,
reappearing, disappearing, returning.

Huihui
Taumarunui 2014

'Well kids, I'm going fishing.' Out of the car
and straight to the confluence, goes Joe
in his camo waders. A jet boat is launching
at the ramp into the Ōngarue,

a sound that wipes out all other sound,
then blares into the distance.
Another dry summer has ended
with weeks of rain.

Ōngarue is opaque, mud-and-shit
coloured. Poplar leaves float on its surface;
big, round and yellow, like fantastical coins.
Joe steps into Whanganui,

the other prong of the fork. The water answers yes
to all of Mountain Safety's unsafe-to-cross criteria:
it is moving faster than you can walk;
it is above your knees; you can't see the bottom.

Three women glide past in kayaks, stern-faced,
intent on something. Another jet boat.
It is all we can do to stop the children plunging in,
boots and all. Under a bandage

on Felix's arm are grazes, and a puncture
through to the fat, from a chance encounter
with a hungry kunekune. Arm up to the elbow
swallowed into that hot, earthy maw.

As we spread our picnic on the stones,
a wasp stings Lukas under his lip:
with every wail it swells a little more.
We drive out past the sports club: *Home of the Eels*,

Ngapuwaiwaha marae,
Ngahuihuinga community gardens,
the old name for Cherry Grove.
Huihui: to gather. Like water does.

II. A BODY OF WATER

Wherever I live, let me come home to you
As you are, as I am, where you
Meet me and walk with me to the river.

—Marilyn Hacker, 'Going Back to the River'

Among the murk I will find things to worship . . .

—John Kinsella, *The New Arcadia*

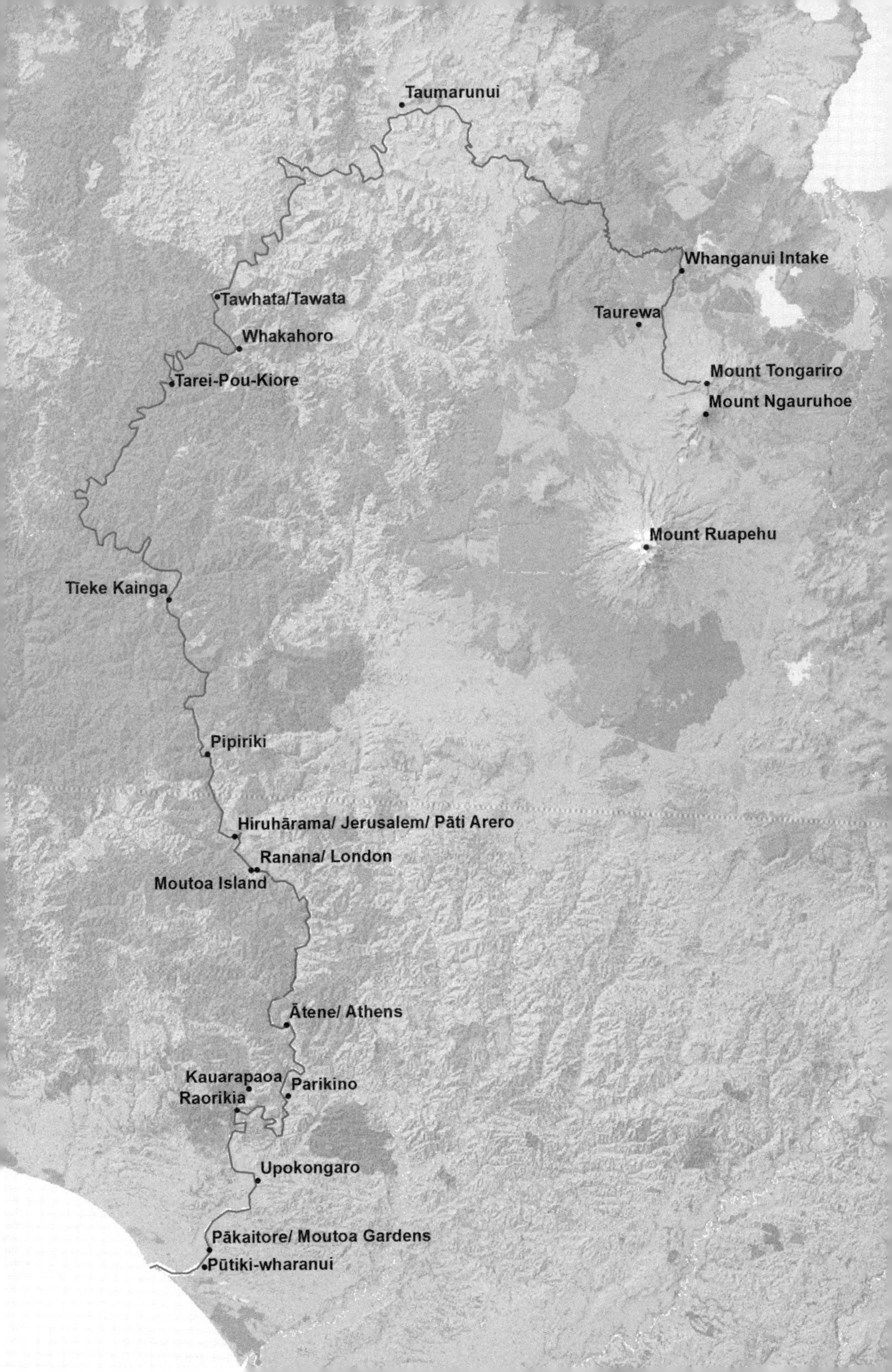

Taumarunui
Whanganui Intake
Taurewa
Tawhata/Tawata
Whakahoro
Tarei-Pou-Kiore
Mount Tongariro
Mount Ngauruhoe
Mount Ruapehu
Tīeke Kainga
Pipiriki
Hiruhārama/ Jerusalem/ Pāti Arero
Ranana/ London
Moutoa Island
Ātene/ Athens
Kauarapaoa
Parikino
Raorikia
Upokongaro
Pākaitore/ Moutoa Gardens
Pūtiki-wharanui

Puanga

The children are making the river.
They have sand and pumice. They have ferns.

A teacher unrolls masking tape,
presses a map to the wall.

There are birds that sing when squeezed.
Wild-eyed, a girl clings to a tūī.

There are little whare, into which
the birds can be inserted.

A boy carries the kōkako
around all morning.

*

Over the radio, silence.
Then the swish of piupiu,

tread of feet,
pat of plastic poi.

Stillness. Silence moves
across the airwaves.

A drum, a guitar strum
breaks it. Girls open their throats.

The sound of lungs filling.
The loosing of tongues.

*

This is Puanga, or Rigel.
The laser pointer circles the gleam.

Children's heads silhouetted
by the projector,
continually in movement.

This is Matariki, or the Pleiades,
or Subaru.

But in Whanganui,
Puanga is the star
we look for in the new year.

*

The children have made star biscuits.
They have harakeke. They are weaving stars.

Milo in the star-cave,
telescopes searching cloud.

They have playdough the colour
of night sky, filled with glitter.

Dressing gowns, gumboots, woolly hats.
A brazier in the sandpit.

The smell of damp air.
The smell of burning sugar.

*

It is a time for planting.
A child chooses a pine

with blue-grey needles.
It will bear nuts in forty years.

A time for gathering.
Pink yam fingers poke from the soil.

A time to prepare new ground.
Bared black of loam.

Where can we plant this tree?
Where will it cast its shadow?

*

From here, Puanga.
From here, Rigel.

In the sky a hunter stands
on his hands,
both feet upwards.

In a tank a real eel.
The silver of īnanga.

The stones are lined up,
the birds are positioned.
The children are making the river.

Snow
Huka mātahi—the first snowfall

The first snow falls
like sugar, sown
breath-thin
on each blank mountain's face.
The rock
pricked
apart by needling ice
like shattered bone
bears
down, and wears
down to fine scree.
Melt water sucks
below,
and percolates
through every crevice, laced
by weave of gravity,
a plaited rope to tether.

Now leisure calls,
now move the stone,
begin
to smooth every space,
the shock
slicked,
each surface swept nice.
Fresh powder blown
glares
white, the chairs
ascending lee.

The rumbling trucks
let go
their loaded weights
in oblong waste-piles, placed
for regularity,
to meet the winter weather.

The cold enthralls,
the crowds are known
to win
their pleasure on this place.
The flock
flicked
to sloping paradise,
the glowing cone
shares
itself, wares
spread out to see.
From spills and shucks
a floe
of waste awaits
the greater thaw, the traced
maps of a century
beneath white flake and feather.

Through zips and ducks
of snow,
through bends and straits,
each tiny move encased
in cold complexity.
Blind cells knock together.

Seed

You are in the wildness, wild with song and honey.
You are in the beak and tongue and claw.
You are in the rock face, weathered by the freeze-thaw,
in the summit sulphurous and stony.
Red grain of wood, wet oozing sap,
domatia where the tiny leaf-mites sleep,
ripe pulpy humus dropped and mashed
by rotting rain, the orange berries flushed
on twigs of foetid plants, the swoop
of water black with tannins in the deep-
cut stream. All live things spill your smell,
all death exudes your taste, and in your fist fits all.

You are in a handle, frothing full of amber,
you are in the barmaid's splashy bosom.
You are in the bar-room talk, its raucous timbre,
currency of towns that die and blossom.
Faux-Swiss hotels of varnished pine,
sloshed maenads arm in arm beneath the moon,
and in the morning on the pale
snow, tourists shouting *Das ist total geil!*
Fluorescent shoes with unspoiled treads,
ovine erotica of clothing ads,
fresh shit of dogs in bread-bags scooped
from foot-tracks gravelled neat and strong, precisely mapped.

Ghost in everything that moves,
shape and map of all that lives,
in your ways of keeping time
lie the marks that ours is come:
what perishes, what thrives.
Here the cork bursts from the bottle,
here are skeletons to rattle.
Wall of sound and thralling silence,
cryptic means to unknown ends,
tremor of a shifting valence,
knife that cuts and tie that binds.
No tale we tell entails your quiet work,
no fight we sweat unveils a major plan
that pins you down from chaos in the dark
or clearly charts the ways that you have been
above, below us flung, around us sown.
Each small thing comes to you in ritual of its own.

Flow

To the stone, to the hill, to the heap, to the seep,
to the drip, to the weep, to the rock, to the rill,
to the fell, to the wash, to the splash, to the rush,
to the bush, to the creep, to the hush;

to the down, to the plain, to the green, to the drift,
to the rift, to the graft, to the shift, to the break,
to the shake, to the lift, to the fall, to the wall,
to the heft, to the cleft, to the call;

to the bend, to the wend, to the wind, to the run,
to the roam, to the rend, to the seam, to the foam,
to the scum, to the moss, to the mist, to the grist,
to the grind, to the grain, to the dust;

to the core, to the gorge, to the grove, to the cave,
to the dive, to the shore, to the grave, to the give,
to the leave, to the oar, to the spring, to the tongue,
to the ring, to the roar, to the song;

to the surge, to the flood, to the blood, to the urge
to the rage, to the rod, to the rood, to the vein,
to the chain, to the town, to the side, to the slide,
to the breadth, to the depth, to the tide;

to the neap, to the deep, to the drag, to the fog,
to the stick, to the slick, to the sweep, to the twig,
to the roll, to the tug, to the roil, to the shell,
to the swell, to the ebb, to the well, to the sea.

Kākahi
Freshwater mussel / Echyridella spp.

The water low,
the run-off thick,
the host-fish sparse,
the shells sealed shut.
Twenty-two sites,
only one fit
to harvest from.
An empty sack.

Western Diversion

Hills must be levelled, the pumice stone crushed to span across
                                                    valleys;
   ninety-five tonnes of machine scrapes at the fracturing rock.
Heads of gigantic proportion working the earth in their mandibles,
   thudding of glistening shaft, pumping through layers of soil.
Deeper and cooler each day the tunnellers travel through darkness,
   over each entrance a shrine, holding a candlelit saint.

Flowering breasts adorning the ceilings of single men's bunkers,
   workshop a splaying of legs, pink and invertebrate form.
Muscle of men in the showers, soap to the ropings of tension,
   face to the sun-hardened towel, shirt to the crick in the back.
Click of the pool cue, sending out sparks over green felted valleys,
   clock of the graveyard shift, bell a rock breaking like sleep.

Fingers of pipework channelling down to the site of the
                                                   powerhouse,
   stroking the clay-bellied hill, poking in ditches of murk.
Working the long job of gouging a channel through desolate
                                                   swampland,
   block by block set in its place, the cuboid symmetrical dam.
Pipe flushing water, a spuming of high-pressure whiteness
   down the rectangular race, wetting the cameraman's lens.

Lichen grows over the culvert, the burgeoning language of fungus,
   cylinder sucking its load, passing obscured into scrub.
What is this twist in the chest, at this dull insignificant concrete?
   If unaware what it took, one wouldn't think to react.
Shoulder whatever you carry, return to the places you plug in,
   no way to cipher this loss, only a socket for void.

Whio
Blue duck/*Hymenolaimus malacorhynchos*

The low guttural groan,
the whistle. How they hone
it, in clear water, pair
judiciously. They wear
a monetary hue.
Hard to come by, that blue.

Map-making

The chain clanking,   the clouds closing
we waded through wetness.   *Waste* is the word for it.
Feeling each footfall,   scenting the foetid
slurry of shrubbery   sliced with the slasher.
The fog had a freshness   I felt through the flannel
cloth of my shirt: it clung to me, clammy.
These places appeared   perpetually sodden,
smelled of a swampy   eternal sameness.
The air had a taste   of toe-toe, tea-tree.
The ground was bogging,   a break in my boot-heel
let in a leak.   I was losing composure.
My throat thirsting,   I thought of tea,
slung off my haversack.   Head down, I heard
my companion calling,   clutching his chest.
I'd never learned   the local language,
wondered at what   he was warning us of.
The rainclouds opened,   a roll of thunder
struck my ears,   the start of a storm.
I looked to where   the lad was pointing,
the drab lagoon   lying below us.
Above the surface   a shape had assembled:
fierce, gargantuan,   galloping at us.
I felt a hotness   heap in my heart-valves,
a jerk, a jump   searing my jugular.
No time to think   of a reasonable theory
explaining its presence,   I picked up my gear
and fled through the flax.   My fellows flung out
in different directions.   I dropped the theodolite;
stumbling to save it,   the slasher sliced
my shin to the bone.   The beast behind me,

I crawled to shelter,   shredded my shirt
and tied a tourniquet   tight on the wound.
My gear gone,   I lay there, gibbering,
crawled for camp,   my cut still oozing.
Two of the trio   had traipsed in before me.
All night we opened   our eyes at each noise.
At dawn we searched   in a deep dread
of finding our friend   flensed and dismembered.
We found him, at length   laid in the swamp,
covered in cuts,   knocked out cold.
He couldn't, or wouldn't   recall his capture
but cleft in his skin   were the marks of claws.
To this day I don't dare   to test my doubts,
retrace the trail   or recover my tools.
Call me a coward   I'll meet your contempt,
I marked a marshland   on the map I made.
Certain places   surveys must circumvent,
most of our maps   leave minutiae omitted.

Shingle beach

Kink in the path
fork of a branch
slub in the cloth
spoonful of salt
knot in the grain
fleck in the skin
grist in the mill
seed in a hull.

To even out
to open space
the stone removed
its roundness cracked.
A straighter course
a blotted spill
a metalled road
a deeper hole.

Trout
Oncorhynchus mykiss
Salmo trutta

He with his flexing
        ray-fins at the ready
she scrapes her redd
        in the bed
                of fine gravel
where water will travel
        in riffle soft-peaking.
Now he moves, sexing
        the roe lying steady
spills his milt, spread
        to the head
                at a level
to let it unravel
        and meet what it's seeking.

Yellow sac'd alevin clustered in hiding
colliding
        together, translucent, light-bending
freckled and blending
        to stone-colour, matching
each roll to the current's tug, latching, unlatching.

Bug-eyed and bulbous, their yolk-spots subsiding,
backsliding
        they break from their cracks to the wending
of current, fast-tending
        to gulping and snatching
grown in the flicker of seek-and-dispatching.

Fingerlings flashing
> in blurring reactions
swift in their shifting,
> > gulp-sifting
> > > and feeding
on scoops of fresh seeding
> > > on small fry, on all things.

Rising and splashing
> to grasp dark refractions
of drowned insects drifting
bob-lifting
> > > black-beading
the surface. A weeding
> > of weakness, of small things.

There was the water, as though it were waiting
creating
> an emptiness, ripe for the taking.
Sport in the making,
> come fry in a swilling
of barrel by cartload. The rivers are filling.

Flies for the flicking, and hooks for the baiting
fixating
> in hunger, slow stares without breaking.
No easy slaking
> this thirst, or this thrilling
the line gathers weight, and the buckets are spilling.

There is a beauty
        in marking a cluster
each to his stone
        wet to bone
                in the pooling
where the wide-spooling
            hook shimmers, dangling.
We have a duty
        to strengthen and muster
keep what's our own
        what we've grown,
                    overruling
anything spoiling
        the pleasures of angling.

That which was here first is caught in the jawing,
the gnawing
    of newness works to uncover.
Seek to recover
    then fall to a culling:
newcomers spread and their numbers keep swelling.

The small and the slimy are fit for ignoring
the roaring
    of rapid calls to the rover.
All the world over
        tales in the telling
Keep travellers coming, each one of them calling,

Saying: Come, fish, break from your hollow
Be rose-moled, be of sufficient weight
to meet your fate
       on the thin line you follow.
Gulp, swallow
       this darting lure, its yearning.
Come to my hook, fish, and keep returning.

Grayling
Upokororo / *Prototroctes oxyrhynchus*

Small, insignificant fish.
Even your name is formless.

Null, extinct, extinguished.
Even your form is homeless.

Spring—black, red and white

The soil, awaiting spade.
Fingerprints of fire.

Light through the walls
of the womb. Capillary. Breath.

Heke—A rib cage.
Maihi—Arms outstretched.

Nights shorten,
the air quickens.

The wind, livid
lifting flags.

*

Poplars bud,
tītoki splits arils.

A black bird
with a russet saddle.

Heavy and bristling, a sow gives birth.
Piglet upon piglet upon piglet.

Rise, fall, rise, fall, rise.
The water breathing.

Are the lamprey still running?
Against the current.

*

Hunter from hill,
forest-fed meat.

Mist—osmosis,
transpiration.
The droplets disperse.

The paper's space.
Fibre of pine.

Ink runs, then
tears.
Wai ora.

*

Volcanic clay,
rubbed with pebbles.

Rust of a kākā
folding its wings.

Fountain pen, printing press.
The glyphs of raupatu.

Things that bleed
when you cut them up.

Mā pango, mā whero
ka oti te mahi.

*

Every tributary.
The wide-mouthed estuary.

A pattern of veins
in brain or breast.

The taut threads
of a plaited rope.

The river
is a person.

It draws
its own maps.

*

Serpentine stone
in an unlit room.

A kōauau
starts up
when no one's around.

Dim linoleum,
faulty electricals.

Museum doors
banging
in the wind.

Kōura
Freshwater crayfish / *Paranephrops planifrons*

Berried with eggs, damp-coloured, decked with spines,
its tail pulled off, still hides between the stones.

Whirlpool
Tarei-pou-kiore

When the river floods the water squeezes
through a cleft between a massive cliff-face
and a mass of boulders, swift and yellow.
At its base a pool too deep to measure,

gaping, sucking, roaring from its gullet
like a hungry monster, caged and pacing
round its walled enclosure, bent on killing.
Past the cliff the twelve-foot waves come rushing.

'Don't go through in high flood,' say the bosses.
'Turn or tie up, wait for it to quieten.'
On the other hand, there's pride in running
services exactly to a schedule.

Cross the beast by charging at its centre;
get a full steam up and make for safety;
keep within arm's reach the only lifebuoy
we possess, in case the skipper fumbles.

Engine flooding, vessel heeling madly,
clinging to the boat's the only option;
though it might go under, no use jumping—
diving in would only kill you quicker.

But then the boat is righted, and flung free
as though the whirlpool spits it in distaste.
Dog-like, it shakes the water from its decks.

Dynamite

Make it wider, make it deep,
blast it away!
Where shingle shifts, where cliffs fall steep,
make it wider, make it deep.
The channel must be smooth as sleep,
let no obstruction stay.
Make it wider, make it deep.
Blast it away!

Fire

God cut a clump   of reddish clay
breathed moist on it   and made a man.
This truth fits neatly   with native knowledge:
they will take to heart   what Taylor teaches.
Scores of souls   must be swiftly saved.
With sons, three cows,   two calves and a mare
he sails from Sydney   by the ship *Nimrod,*
those dear having done   their best to dissuade him.
But a headier call   was heard by him
to leave his enviable   English existence
and go South as sure   as the compass spins
to the worst country   the world owns.
His wife follows   with waxing daughters.
Columbine carries them.   The cruel bar crossed
        they berth
        to forge a house of good
        upon the shaking earth,
        and set to buying wood
        each tree a blanket's worth.

Taylor's mission   takes him tramping
a wet wilderness: along waterways,
sea-coasts, swamps,   wastes and settlements.
No flood, no forest,   no river, no fen
prevents his progress: he pushes all ways.
When he's cramped with the cold   he's carried by guides.
They make their meals   of kākā and mushrooms,
lampreys, potatoes,   plain and unsalted.
Tired from travelling   he tethers his tent,
sealed against rain   with sugar of lead,

then rises early   to rescue the wicked,
baptise the heathen   wed breeders of bastards
(fifty-two bonds   tied before breakfast),
hands to the dying   hope of heaven.
Ever searching   for souls to bring
        ashore,
        he hears a dying chief
        call for an end to war
        in spite of old belief
        and what has gone before.

As he wends his way   he writes his works
on botany, minerals,   bones of birds
as large as elephants   lying in caves.
A broker of peace,   he pulls teeth,
lances abscesses,   lectures on hygiene,
gives salt to women   seeking sorcery
to silence their claims   of his seeming stinginess,
frowns on the fierce   facial tattoos,
the rotten corn   rank and reeking.
And near to his home   gives new names:
Hiona, Ātene,   Hiruhārama
Raorikia,   Ramahiku
Karatia, Ranana: Christian cities
made malleable   for Māori speakers.
        In time
        the old names surface less,
        the church bells sound their chime
        to summon and to bless
        the work of the sublime.

Peace cannot prevail   all times and places
and like a lash   of Catholic lightning
comes Father Lampila   the fiery Frenchman
who girds hills green   and grows grapes,
who feeds his flock   and filches souls,
whose *Hine Roimata*   holding her hands out
weeps tears of sap   and speaks in whispers.
Who challenges Taylor: Let truth be chosen
by trial of fire: who's freed from the flames
is God's true missionary   given His grace
to prove His power   and serve His purpose.
The fire alight,   the sparks leaping,
Taylor refuses   and takes to the track.
Lampila's friends   pull him free of the flames,
in spite of his vices   crown him the victor,
a thousand Catholics   swiftly converted.
> The loss
> will never be returned
> and now upon the cross
> the Priest who would have burned
> hangs his unseemly dross.

Bishop Selwyn   heads south from Auckland
travelling on foot   through hidden territory.
To meet with him,   Taylor makes for the mountains.
They camp in rain   with the rivers rising;
to ford the surge   they must strip to the skin
and cross with their clothes   carried on their heads.
The Bishop wades   the wild waters,
Taylor is carried,   Mr Cotton floats
aboard the Bishop's   inflatable bed.
Nihil tries to ford   but is swept off his feet.

They camp after crossing   and catch a wild cat,
the meat they crave   being duly cooked.
The following day   it's tūī and fern-root,
weka with rice   and wild potatoes.
Procuring a pig,   Taylor fries some pork.
His heart is happy   but his head is aching.
In the morning he presses   for Pipiriki,
>   no one
>   to keep him company.
>   The Bishop's work is done;
>   he paddles for the sea
>   along the river run.

The wilderness years   wearing on him,
he breaks for business   back in England
taking Chief Hoani   Wiremu Hipango
to gift her Majesty   cloaks and mere.
Winds back round the world   on the *Lancashire Witch*.
When stopped on the island   of Saint Helena
for water and stores,   a weeping willow
is sighted growing   on the grave of Napoleon.
He plucks off a sprig,   puts it in his pocket.
Mrs Taylor keeps it   with care in her cabin,
on bright days brought out   in its medicine bottle.
Planted at Pūtiki,   it becomes the parent
of weeping willows   way up Whanganui.
Wherever he travels,   he takes a few twigs,
sets them to root   in the river silt.
>   They grow
>   a beacon of smoke-green
>   so travellers might know
>   where Taylor's feet have been
>   wading into the flow.

At Christmas the church   at Pūtiki is crowded
with Christian Māori   come to the call
while over the river   the rush to the races
keeps the Pākehā   apart from his preacher.
Settlers seek his assistance,   but seldom support him,
and progress is slow,   necromancy persistent.
Locals cling to old customs   like working unclothed.
One day old Ake   is digging his garden
when Taylor commands him   to put on a mat.
In the struggle to shove   the man out of sight,
his coat is ruined   with the ripe red clay
that Ake has spread   all over his skin,
        to shade
        it from the heat of day,
        his sacredness displayed.
        A man cut out of clay
        just as his God had made.

His years waning,   Taylor carries on writing,
filling his journals   with figures and sketches.
His second son   succeeds him as Reverend,
leaves him at leisure   to learn his sciences,
continue collecting   his native curios.
The cluster of conflict   becomes a town,
the roads fill,   the fold increases,
the settler's graveyard   gathers its citizens.
And when in kindness   God calls him close
he is laid to rest   in a sandy rise
a place that looks over   to Pūtiki-wharanui.

From there
his living friends can hold
Te Teira in their care
the stories he has told
still moving in the air.

Hīnaki

Open O each end of the ovoid net,
funnelled, bent back, dark with tannin stain,
hung in a glass case over a model weir,
though where the poles remain the traps are set,
your cup will never hold an eel again.
Amidst your star-weave, small stones still adhere.

Tuna
Longfin eel / *Anguilla dieffenbachii*

They taper their heads, enlarge their eyes, and swim downstream
far out to breeding grounds in the Pacific. Where these lie
no one really knows. They spawn and then they die.
The leaf-shaped larvae drift the currents, turn to glass eels once
                                                          they're home.

Foundlings

The doctor was walking the wharves. A cry
sounded in his arms. He handed me one
newborn, nameless boy, knowing that I

would not refuse. We named this first son
Joseph March, saint and month. Our flock expands:
bundles found on steamboats. In Wellington

the harbour is never full. A girl who stands
astride the rocks, at Oriental Bay
carries a swaddled boy. Unbid, my hands

move up to take him. I hear myself say
Tell me your name, and it remains with me.
The boy is baptised Francis, on his way

up country to the hill-bound nursery
at Hiruhārama, the mud and dust
of our farm on the middle Whanganui.

Why should a woman's name be lost for lust?
Mercy and secrecy do well together;
rather than hide and starve, a girl can entrust

her child to good care, and be free to tether
her loose ends from the fray, to show her face
in the world again. In rough or fine weather

Hiruhārama always has more space.
Each foundling is a child of God, the brother
or sister of Him for whom there was no place

in the inn. Even in the arms of its mother
it has no room. The sisters are its aunts,
myself, Mother Joseph, its grandmother,

and in our quiet mission there's a chance
at a worthy life. Children tend to bees,
cows, horses and the vegetable plants,

and in the orchard the thousand cherries;
making music with a kerosene tin,
the littlies scare the blackbirds from the trees.

Black cherries, sweetheart cherries, stain the chin
of the boy with his packhorse, slow, unsure,
climbing the steep track to bring the milk in.

In the farmhouse kitchen, with its earthen floor
we cook hearth-fire cakes, while the King of Kings
stands in his watching place behind the door.

Our days are given up to humble things,
searching in the bush for leaves, bark, roots, shoots
to make our medicines. In the dark evenings

we often clean and waterproof our boots
with tallow, beeswax, lard and olive oil
warmed on the fire. The candles blown, night mutes

the valley, only the trampling pigs spoil
the depth of silence. At nine, we all sleep.
Then, rising shy of five, resume our toil.

Most days, there's nothing I can do to keep
our Father Soulas from his morbid bent.
He lives beside that figure come to reap

his share of souls, and all his days are spent
anticipating death, the timbers sawn
for coffins for himself, myself, intent

on little else. Still more babies are born
and brought to us. Our convent is inspected,
but no money given, because we warn

the authorities we can't be expected
to name the childrens' mothers. Still I write
to Parliament, but my pleas are rejected.

All I can do is wander in the night,
and pray Our Lady will fill me with her light.

Lamprey
Piharau / *Geotria australis*

Swam up at the side,
a sweet meat clad
in a grey like mud.

Moutoa

A minor island.
A rough-shaped diamond.
A node of greenness,
of things unspoken.
Bare wilding poplars.
Gorse-blaze and lupin.
Its peaceful aspect,
its shifting outline.

Summer

You must've stunk, musky, skunky hippie
walking up the road to Jerusalem.

Your bare feet pressed the dust,
like it would always be summer.

Heat shimmered over the verges,
ox-eyes shivered in an almost-breeze.

What magnet pulled you?
Love is not a recent thing.

Bees did waggle-dances,
wood beetles sang in the empty house.

*

The thousand curves in the old bus,
the walk through nauseous groves.

But I don't *want* to see
a blue duck, whines a child.

Youth stretched in the grass,
deep in Dickens.

A girl beside him,
her head strung with beads.

Like a bride who wears
her dowry in her hair.

*

All the life in London:
a wandering piglet.

Dark and lovely
a Greek woman smiles
under the road-sign at Athens.

The convent's florid bedspreads.
Its table under poplars.

My skin's come off,
cries the child in his sleep,
my bones are hanging out.

*

A girl writes the marae names
in her curly script

on the song sheet.
Ehara i te mea, nō ināianei te aroha.

*Hutia te rito o te harakeke
Kei whea te kōmako e kō?*

As scones are served
a woman strums and sings

*Someone loves you, honey
Wherever you go.*

*

You used to hold your arms
out, cruciform,

your long hair hung
around your shoulders.

Beard touching your chest.
Guitar slung over your groin.

The sun has written
lyrics in your skin.

You say you paddled here
from Taumarunui, alone.

*

Everyone who passes
seems to know you, thin traveller.

The spine of the woman
beside you curves,
breast drooping to her child's mouth.

You talk of community,
part ways at the carpark.

It is Christmas.
Kate is waiting for you.
And Mary has a cake in the oven.

Girl with baby in a cornfield
Partington 103a

Turning your head, you stand still, briefly pausing.
Corn rears above you, its green flowers droopy.
Baby lolls over your shoulder—she's sleepy,
tied up in blanket-cloth, tight to you, dozing,
heavy as rock. Then the click of the shutter
startles—the camera completing its gazing.
Moving away, baby's eyelids re-closing,
lulled by the grasshopper's rasp, the birds' patter.

Pandora's Box
Wilkies shell bed

When you come to this cliff,
                       cleared and cut-back,
roughly risen,
            you read in the rock
strangely pertinent
                 Pliocene prophecies
silent for centuries,
            scripted in shells.
Sedimentary facies,
            fossil fauna,
cyclostratigraphy,
            a testable timescale.
Search this shell-script,
            a set of psalms,
a learnable lesson,
          limed, calcareous.
Buried bones,
          busted banks.
Contours, isobars
            cramming closer.
A storm is coming,
            we've searched and seen it
in old oysters,
          opened to weather.

Kauarapaoa

The road climbs up abruptly, here,
beneath the cliff the water dark blue glass.
A peacock dives into the grass—
oh where oh where oh where oh where oh where?
Wet tang of sheep shit, mass of trees
releasing plant-scents in the angled sun,
those smells of summers been and gone,
bruised sap, ripe humus, rising to the nose.
The road bends with the deep-cut stream,
leaves fuzz the chasm to its brim,
and the stream slinks down towards the river
like a lover you'll never get over.

All over, loose exotic scrub:
gum, willow, wattle, elder, poplar, broom
stitching the hillside like a seam
across the rends of slip-soil dull and drab.
A man in white bends to his hives
below a face of mānuka sprayed dead.
Sheep crawl amongst the sticks to feed
on threads of green, wherever greenness lives.
Across the road, like greying bones
lie slash-piles of cut-over pines.
And the naked peaks roll on forever
like a lover you'll never get over.

A falcon calls above the rise:
Kek kek kek kek kek kek kek kek kek kek.
Far over farmland lies a break
of ocean, and the pale of western skies.
The white volcano points out north,
seeming steadfast, despite its restless sleep.
The road skirts, in a gravel loop
a drop so steep it catches in the breath.
The roadside bluffs divulge their shells,
reveal the ocean held these hills.
And water is as much a mover
as soil in softness is a giver.
And what can the land do but take cover?
Like a lover you'll never get over.

Children in the mud
Three mothers

I
The pang, the push, the slide,
the stretch, the yawning wide,

your supple form uncurled
into the waiting world

and water was your guide.
You learned its turn and tide,

you learned its rage and calm.
The bank-mud was your balm,

as back and forth you swam,
and back and forth you swam.

II
I gave you as sacrifice to the sea.
Pregnant, mad, no help for me.

You were four, disobedient, wild.
I said to the flood-tide: hold my child.

They found your body washed ashore
just south. Came knocking at my door.

Took me to die by the hangman's noose.
I pleaded womb: they turned me loose.

I'll carry you until my death.
The current in my every breath.

III
Down by the marketplace we often walked.
My friend and I stood on the wharf, and talked.

The tide was out, the bed exposed to day.
You leaped the boardwalk into mud, to play.

All four went out light-footed on the beach.
I ran to you; you ran beyond my reach.

I didn't know if you would sink or float.
The tang of panic rising in my throat.

My knee-high boots sank knee-deep in the scum.
I called and called; you laughed, and wouldn't come.

Wattlebirds

There were those who'd seen them, moving like ghosts,
heard their calls, deeper, deeper in the wastes
of scrub, slash, forest. The numbers smaller
as time passed, each tale dying with its teller.

Pākaitore

They formed a circle, holding hands.
What cop would break such brittle wrists
stretched round this smallest of small lands?

The statue gone, the plinth still stands.
The fig tree squiggles, bends and twists.
Its branches circle, holding hands.

Some years the garden fills with bands.
The vocals roll, the beat insists,
all round this smallest of small lands.

Movers and shakers, firebrands,
rock standing firm, song that resists;
all in that circle, holding hands.

The grassy bank, the river sands,
the landing place that still exists
beside this smallest of small lands.

The years move on, and time expands
the distance, but the tale persists:
they formed a circle, holding hands,
around this smallest of small lands.

Flood

Riverbank mum:
They came and told us *clear out.* It got late.
We packed enough,
drove to my folks, nothing to do but wait
to check our stuff.
I never dreamed this happening to me.
Like TV or the movies, but to see
our home gone, stings.
My family's things
buried in mud like we were nobody.

Hill country farmer:
You had any damage? How about you?
Our roads are locked,
washed-out, or slipped. Loaders are inching through
each bend that's blocked.
The power's out, the pump is off, that means
no showers. We'll survive on tinned baked beans.
Plenty of wood.
We can make good
out here, till rescue intervenes.

Flood:
Did you imagine I'd go wide as this?
Lap up your streets?
The lumpen stopbanks easy to dismiss;
where water meets
tarmac is where things really start to flow.
I waste whatever's lying low,
rip up your pontoons, wharves, unmoor your boats.

My ample stomach swiftly bloats
with free and flash,
treasure and trash
whatever I work loose, whatever floats.

Valley dweller:
Ah well that's it for me, we're walking out.
Goodbye, mud-hole.
The missus's had enough. This latest clout
straight to the soul
straw to the camel. All our worldly worth
strewn round this muddy, mangled square of dearth.
Take stock of it,
pile up our shit,
and find another piece of earth.

Kowhai Park brontosaurus:
My hump is all you'll see above the murk.
An octopus
submerged at last, arches lime-green leg-work.
Enveloped thus,
the grey whale drinks Its hollow insides full.
Tongue moulded to the earth, staunch as a bull,
I brace my neck.
The sunken wreck
of playground bears the river's pull.

Flood:
Into your very fabric I will seep.
So let it pour.
Into your halls and offices I'll creep,
breach every door.

I pop the lids of sewers, make them spume,
I enter every pleasant room
all bitter, spewy, indiscriminate.
Congeal all with my aggregate
of silt and stick,
of faecal slick,
choke up your holes and leave you desperate.

Road-clearing volunteers:
All over, rubberneckers getting stuck.
They'll never learn.
If they want help then they're shit out of luck,
no room to turn.
Why don't they help *us,* bring a shovel down,
instead of being a nuisance to the town.
While others hurt,
they gawk for sport.
Drowning in mud? Well, let them drown.

Plateau lifestyler:
Peak flow 4.8 kilotonnes per second,
time to reflect.
A tenth of that was soil, or so I reckoned.
Where's the respect?
It's bleeding harder than land can sustain.
Truckloads of our best asset down the drain.
Arabs have oil,
but we have soil.
At least, we did. We won't, again.

Flood:
What seemed safe isn't, what you thought stood still
is fraught with flux.
There is a wilding horse in every hill
that rears and bucks.
You live astride two moving chunks of crust:
fire, wind, earth, water, spark and dust,
this young geology is supple-sewn.
It answers to your blood and bone,
but strip it bare:
you must prepare.
I'll be the worst that you have ever known.

Girl with oranges

You stand there, shifting on your feet,
you push your hair out of your eye.
Your trestle set beside the street,
your gaze set at the lower sky.
You've built your orange-stall beside the river.
You're younger than you look, or are you older?
Well, it's one way to lose a lonely hour.

You seem to shimmer in the heat,
a candle or a butterfly.
Your orange letters round and neat
your orange dress all flowery.
Although the day is warm you seem to shiver;
beneath the spreading trees the air is colder.
Is it their big-limbed presence makes you cower?

The customers you shyly greet
are few and far between; you sigh.
The traffic is an ageing fleet
of wrecks in souped-up finery.
A different destination for each driver:
new tavern-bound, to drink an anger bolder,
or to the cemetery, to lay a flower.

Regardless, each moves on up-street
through weather-boarded blocks that lie
in cut-out grid, calm and complete
in their peculiar symmetry.
The smoke-free dairy makes as much as ever.
The absent landlords leave their flats to moulder.
The pirate station's fist is raised to power.

In all the kitchens flour is poured, each siever
pausing to inhale the scents, to shoulder
longings. So they stir it, bitter, sour.

Spoonbill
Kōtuku ngutupapa / *Platalea regia*

Down by Bullocks' yards, where piles of bark
and boulders, fill and gravel bide their time,
the waders crept, once sewage was removed.

The tidal mud grew sweeter—coffee-dark
of water faded honey-pale. The slime,
thinned out, held feasts, the wide beaks clapped and roved.

Listen

Now here we are, treading water through time.
Shoulders set with all the things it's ripe to
take into account. Now we can listen
for the slow push of mud, its murky truth
under the current. Face the roundabout
mirror, which is ready to reflect us.

A lapsed lens doodles light, a this-is-us
free calendar, with blocky squares of time.
What does anyone really know about
the strata we're in, sedimented to
the layers below, not in them. The truth
is only sometimes spoken. Still. Listen.

Dead premier drinking your beer, listen.
The river you're in is one that cuts us
through. Rolling in the thick bed, headless, truth
disjoints you. On the bank, tram tracks mark time,
a vintage daydream easy to succumb to,
still, with the sense of things not talked about.

The shock-jockey, jogging, bounces about
like a wild goat. His feet stamp—don't listen.
The dead mayor wakes in the night, hearkens to
leaf music. He shakes with fear: *them or us!*
The cops are ready. Some wounds even time
has trouble stitching up, some grains of truth

will sit beneath the skin for years. The truth
turns up at odd times, between lines about
more digestible things. Sound of this time
is sound of people talking. To listen
through the white noise won't be easy for us.
These dials—what frequencies will they turn to?

The train steams over the bridge; it has to.
The steamboat under it, making a truth
of sumptuous smoke. A photograph of us
is a photograph of bridges, about
to reach respective other sides. Listen,
ear to ground, for lightning earthing. Through time.

There's something troubling 'us'. The letters to
the editor, the time-worn claims to truth.
We've talked about it. Now we should listen.

Autumn

The young man is listening to the river.
Headphones on, behind the bookshelves.

Out come the sounds of spent years.
Out come the voices laid down.

Hands holding branches,
silver under leaves.

*There are some areas
we fought for . . .*

The fuzzy scrawl of a spray-can.
The curve of a cop's helmet.

*

A man drives past the library,
three dogs and two cats in the back.

The shakes in his wrists,
the sun on his neck.

Rain comes and the hills resume
their seasonal slumping.

Hens stop laying, gullies
darken with mud.

Children squeeze hail in their mittens,
yelping.

*

Gourds are strung in the slash,
green and bulbous.

Warts swell on the French pumpkins,
bean pods blacken,
kamokamo thicken their skins.

The buns rise best on Sunday
because Christ rose again.

If the shearer's cook
makes green jelly
it means it will rain.

*

Two thousand years since the last eruption
a steady supply of pumice continues.

Broken reeds floating,
a flat rugby ball, a gatepost acorn.

Beautifully inked, a man
drags a kahawai from the water.

A branch catches in the paddlewheel.
A row of seagulls settle.

The white streaks on the fig tree
look like bat shit, but are bleeds of sap.

*

Stone by stone
the monument is rebuilt.

Chunks of shellrock sprayed
with fluoro yellow numbers.

Mortar carried up the scaffold
in bright orange buckets.

The standard chain
is wearing into dirt.

Has the moving earth
narrowed its two brass bolts?

*

Anzac wreaths laid
on the colonial lion.

The awa station plays
a song about Rua Kenana:
Told his people not to go to war.

While Calbuco blows up,
Ruapehu is orange, serene.

The stone soldier's face is calm
as the crane dangles him
above his rock.

III. THE MOVING SAND

The real issue, of course, was this: atomically, energetically,
everything was wave function. And a wave continues forever into space,
the wavelength never alters, only the intensity lessens, so
in the worst cosmic way everything is connected by vibrations.
And this, as even a dog would know, is no consolation.

—Luke Davies, 'Totem Poem'

O what O what will
Bring us back to
Shore,
        the shore

—George Oppen, *Discrete Series*

Geology

Sea nicked the gently tilted peneplain,
deposited a pebbly sand veneer.
Uplift exposed it. Ash clouds spread their dust;
sand dunes advanced across the coastal flats
and buried them. When sand stopped, land was planed,
coast worn back, valleys shaped. The lines of cliffs
were cut by waves, small stones laid at their feet.
More uplift, more ash spreading, rivers worn
deep into valleys. And the moving sand
rolled in again, was planed, uplifted, cut,
and pumice-showers spilled alluvium.
And all this time the wind blew from the north.
And all this time the wind blew from the west.
And all this time the black sand moved inland.

The long wait

Landing here, Kupe said we must eat the wind.
There was so little food to be found.
They followed the river inland
to a turning place, where Arapawa drowned.

Tīeke, kōkako, tīwaiwaka
were the only signs of life.
Keeping an eye out for the waka,
we waited for them, in the sand-chafe,

and it was a long, long wait.
The river opened its mouth wide,
swallowed, spat. No two times the same.

In a dream, I sat there. It was getting late.
Stranded and unstranded by the surging tide.
To make the water safer, we gave it a name.

Surprise

I carried in my hold this place's price.
They laid it on the Pākaitore mud.
Jew's harps, umbrellas, muskets, nightcaps, red
wool blankets, pencils, camp-stoves, piece by piece.
Then, homai no homai, in the same space
the locals laid their baskets, a fat breed
of pigs, fresh-killed. My crew were duly fed,
the land thought theirs. My work went on, apace.

I'd sailed the southern strait, sick-making sea
pounding my decks. And here, had crossed the bar
time after time, with all eyes on the break,
the flat deceptive calm. Then one spring day
I passed a notch askew, and keel to spar
was shattered in the foam, an utter wreck.

Beachcombing along the tidal reaches

Mud laced by snails, tide mark pocked with crab holes.

Bleached bones of last year's bloated cow fanned out.

From over the flat water sounds a phone
from somewhere a persistent rumbling comes.

How slick and still the water's surface is,
how hushed its slopping sounds against the rim
of shattered shellrock, concrete, tyres, laid out
in failed attempt to force the river's shape.

The push of current finds out every pore.

A lark is singing, perching on a thorn.
I walk to where the rotten slipways stand
and look across the estuary, to see
Taranaki set upon a warehouse
like a chunk of dirty polystyrene.

Lieutenant

It is a rather pleasant place to live.
The only drawback is the horrid sand,
which blows all day and night with no reprieve,
forced into nook and cranny by the wind.
Even the very weave of my white shirts
is infiltrated with dark grains, like mould.
Any scrupulous person in these parts
must change his linen twice a day. I held
out hopes to grow a garden, for a while.
The black sand swallowed up my every seed.
And though the air is cleansing, I still feel
a proper beach should have white sand, a crowd
of picnickers, an even drift of shells,
rows of striped tents, and girls with parasols.

Open Country

White smoke was seeping from a high steel pipe,
milk water blending into sky, on top
of Open Country. At the butcher's shop
fibreglass cattle stood within the swipe
of salt, paint flaking from their rumps. A type
of rotten wind blew over town—the drop
of tonnes of rancid fat had brought a stop
to sewage treatment works. The smell was ripe.

I took a left, drove past the bolted doors
of old wool sheds. I used to call around
there, time to time, break up the dragging day.
They swallowed piles of junk, those sweeping floors,
high roofs. I thought of wheels, thought of the sound
they make when spun, and spinning, roll away.

Constable

As we approached the wharves I fired my gun
to tell them law and order had arrived.
I walked to find the magistrate, through fern
and flax—a swamp. The path to where he lived
I might have called a road, if I had been
a pig. I came upon a shabby man
digging his patch, his clothing rough and worn.
I asked, 'Old chap, where is your master, then?'
'I have none,' he replied. I stared at him.
He smiled and said, 'I'm Samuel King, *Esquire*.'
He told me I could make his tent my home,
and cook some bacon and potatoes there.
I did as bid. The food was plain, and good.
Already on my knees, I thanked my God.

Eunice

There was no set when *Eunice* met her fate.
The vessel struck the bar, the crew reached shore.
This court's opinion is we can't ignore
the fact the captain, first mate, second mate,
and four more of the crew were foreign-born.
No British ship should be allowed to be
so officered and manned. This travesty
might well have been prevented, and I warn
that in these far from normal times more care
must be employed. There should be a return
stating the number of unnaturalised
seamen engaged in coastal shipping. Where
the causes of this wreck lie, now we learn
steering was at fault. I am not surprised.

PechaKucha

I am going to share with you the town I come from.
For years I didn't want to tell anyone. When you drive
in, on the highway there's this sign: Welcome Home.
And I get this sinking feeling, every time I arrive,
that I'll be stuck there forever. Kids have unusual names,
as you can see, reading this slide. My dad's a teacher; it's a list
from a typical class. But we did have some pretty good times:
Durie Hill Tower, Kowhai Park. We used to get pissed
at this lake. This is me on South Beach . . . Oh, the hair,
well it was the 90s, hence my tasselled dolphin sarong.
They made us hold hands in circles, dance around the fire,
or the maypole . . . I have suppressed these memories for so long.
I wanted to be a surfer, catch every gnarly wave.
I wanted to be a boy named Larry, ordinary, but brave.

Mrs Field

I think I would have failed if it were not
for my dear bird, who talked unceasingly,
his cage upon my shoulder. By the sea
were miles of grassy dunes; no shade. The lot
of all our worldly goods my husband got
into a heavy swag; the pots for tea,
our bedding and our clothes. Strapped on to me
my son was bundled like a native tot.
The week-long walk it seemed that every wind
on earth was passing here—a constant threat.
My body sheltered boy and parrot both.
The sand abraded me till I felt skinned
alive. Come evening, we'd make camp, and with
a stick I'd dig up grubs to feed my pet.

Shifting sand

Ninety-eight per cent of scientists claim an increased incidence
of extreme weather events. Carbon emission increases climate
                                                      change.
Using diesel fuel to move sand to the windward is the ultimate
                                          in ignorance
and human arrogance. The amount it costs the council—it's
                                            strange.
Once a year before Christmas they do a major groom,
push huge amounts of sand into the Tasman Sea.
The giant parking lot is empty ninety-nine per cent of the time.
'Eco-thrifty' means you invest upfront and save energy,
save money and help the environment. What I call win–win–win
situations. When you engage in eco-design you just observe
how does nature do it. They're spending lots of money to maintain
something people don't use. Bad design is expensive,
monetarily and carbon-wise. Flood protection is a parallel.
When a hundred-year flood becomes a fifty-year flood, stopbanks
                                                 will fail.

The jail house

We built our local jail house at no cost.
When any sawyer erred against the law
I had him fined in timber—first he lost
to us one hundred board feet, and if more
wrongdoing occurred, two hundred. And so on.
Nobody needed jailing, so to keep
it occupied, I bought a dozen ton
of pumpkins, and potatoes. Where I sleep,
I left clear, and my desk—the rest was filled
up to the roof. It had a homely scent.
One day out shooting at the heads—I'd killed
three ducks—I spied the *Catherine Johnson*, bent
into the western wind. They heard me hail,
brought me on board. We went to see my jail.

Holiday Park

Our second day is the first thing I remember.
We all went down to the beach, and it was like
real windy, and it seemed to go forever. Mum and Dad
used to let us roam around the camp and stuff.

The Spittal brothers didn't like my Dad.
There was this one night, I remember
there were six guys, they tried to like stab him and stuff.
We called the cops. The cops came, and they were like

it's lucky they had two knives in each hand, more stuff
would have happened if they'd had one. Dad's
wrist got broken. They hit him with a baseball bat. And like
this other time, there were these people I remember

they like threw bottles at the house. And they had bats and stuff
as well. And I remember crying to Mum, 'I'm too young to not
                                              have a dad!'

Stormbird

She struck the mole bow-on. I heard the cry
'Make for the shore!' The swell tipped Fireman Kyle
out of his bunk. We dressed—Logan and I
were first to make the wall. Waited a while,
five others also leaped, Kyle stayed on board.
'For God's sake, jump!' I yelled, but was ignored.
Miscalculating, Hunter landed short
and drowned. We saw his body float, and thought
the rest of them were lost, but by the light
of a blue flare, we spied them in the sea:
they clung on to the capsized hull all night.
A sweeping wave tore Kyle and Hinchey free;
the others lived. They took us somewhere warm.
The bodies washed up southwards in the storm.

Bluffs

Jeez, that Kaimatira pumice, man.
It's fucking huge. It's just, how the fuck
did that happen? It would have gone
all the way up to Auckland. The cutting-back
of the road has exposed these beautiful strata.
It came from Mangakino, would have been
a stupendous eruption. The data
shows there's been quite a few eruptions. The crust is thin
here. And most of the planet is 4.2 k under the sea.
If something fell to earth from space, chances are
it'd land under water, 4.2 k down. In a way
the forces have conspired to make sure
that on a planet covered in water, there's some dry land.
If we weren't in an orogeny . . . Well, never mind.

Heads Road

While you were working nightshift out at Mars
Petcare, you had a rented house near here.
Your shifts pinned on the wall: these patterned bars
of shocking pink. Something going somewhere
is what I think of, in that part of town.
'Bits are still coming out of me,' you said.
Beside the mantel, flat-packed, facing down
a pram lay in its box. We drank cheap red
wine, and ate nachos. On the tabletop
a singing caterpillar—a coloured row
of different types of music. You pressed ROCK:
Orange orange orange orange. Then pop,
opera, baroque. Each press a double shock:
early for buying, late for letting go.

Blood and sand

I spy the boat beached on the shore,
its crew crouched at a smutty fire.

We've hunted half the island for
the captain who is standing there.

Joe Rowe. Down south, we saw his goods.
The moko on our people's heads.

He heard us weep. He stood and laughed.
He heard us beg for them. He scoffed.

Now, here he is. 'What's in your boat?'
I climb inside. He pulls me out.

I meet his eyes, and think of smoke.
I touch the club beneath my cloak.

I watch the veins rise in his neck.
I watch him take his last few breaths.

Gathering the berries of *Pimelea turakina*

You couldn't wield a pair of secateurs
to save yourself. And what use is a man
of unsure grip? But still, that soft hand-span
enters my thoughts, down where the ocean blurs
the land, repeatedly. The hot sand stirs
under our feet; we climb to where the tan
of pīngao, grey of marram holds what can
be held. We're silent, and the wind concurs.

We have no grip on time, we haven't seen
how it can wear us down. And at the turn
of season you are gone. The afternoon
is broken, all the places we have been,
and lying in the sun I only burn.
I think I hear days clicking as they prune.

Meat workers

There is a kind of skill in how you cut
the belly of the sheep, and let it spill
its insides, quickly dropping out the gut.
If they don't break our bones, they'll break our will.

My puku not yet sunk from number five
I start my shifts at six, each day a bill
or rent to work for. Somehow I arrive.
If they don't break our bones, they'll break our will.

Then one day I turn up, and we're locked out.
The bosses tell the union, back down, chill,
there's nothing doing kicking shit about.
If they don't break our bones, they'll break our will.

So here we are, out marching in the street.
They've stopped our pay, but they can't stop our feet.

Port Bowen

The line went taut. My hand spun on the reel.
No fish, all snag. I waded to the shore.
On board, the wireless rasped about the war.
They had me there by nights, guarding the steel
that they were slowly breaking up. By feel
I took my footsteps through the surf, its raw
cold burning on my skin. One arm's length more
I'd have my jig, my chance to land a meal.

The moon was in the cloud. Her face all pale
and fuzzed, she dimmed and brightened over the hulk.
And as I searched a wave crept up on me,
a sudden smack. I staggered in its bulk,
went under, thrashed my limbs to no avail.
Come into me, I'll have you, said the sea.

Glow in the dark

Greet me you red-haired ghost, walking tonight
along the riverbank, your mind aflame
with all that can be said, and can't. The fight
of words was always in you, and your name
is said aloud with reverence now. Near here
is where you lived, for the short space of time
you worked the local paper, where the fear
of too much truth, and your unmarried womb
with child, spilled out and took your job with it.
They whispered behind hands, but they were plumb
afraid of all your pluck. Show, blaze and spit!
At nightfall things speak, that by day are dumb.
The cracked sticks burn to ember, smoke and spark.
A small dog's eyes are glowing in the dark.

Longshore drift

Sandfly, Imp, Black Warrior, John Penn, Sturt . . .
The local optimists begin to dream
a future, in the river, for a port.
Prince Alfred, Star of China, Tyne, Midge, Gem . . .
Strong walls need to be built, to save the spit
south of the river mouth, also to form
a buffer for the clay bluffs, and divert
the current. From a quarter mile downstream
of the town bridge, they sink the shellrock in,
drive down the posts. And carefully they dredge
ten thousand cubic yards of silt. But soon
the river floods and fills it up again.
North of the wall, along its rubbly edge,
the sand piles up, the dunes come marching down.

The sandhill

The sand blew from the sea mile upon mile
The black sand came in waves mile upon mile
And shaped itself into an oval hill.

There was a stockade built there, and a well
A loopholed timber stockade, and a well
That watered all the rough shacks on the hill.

They built a sturdy gallows on the hill
They tied four sturdy nooses on the hill
And hanged four captive men till they hung still.

Years later they were digging in the hill
Found four skeletons, buried in the hill
Smashed them with spades and threw them in the fill.

There is a wet place, where thick grass has grown.
The old well oozes up through sand and bone.

Observatory

Kids, who wants to look up through the telescope?
This is the largest unmodified refractor telescope in use
in New Zealand. Birthday girl, you first. I hope
you'll see a planet up there, with rings. That might come loose
if you fiddle with it, be careful. It looks like smoke?
That would be a cloud. Is that *really* a planet? Yes.
Nah, I stuck a picture up on the end. That was a joke.
Could an asteroid destroy humanity? Well, I guess
there's a chance. No object we know of threatens us any time soon.
Is there life like ours, out there? Keep looking up, wave a little.
Parents, bring your kids back one Friday night, maybe the moon
will be visible. Who hasn't had a turn yet? Look there, and it'll
be right in the middle. Ha, that's what everyone says. You
                                            know how
they called this planet Saturn? They really should have named it
                                                Oh wow.

Dead port

Future of the port? Here we go again.
This port is dead. Kaput, lifeless, done.

Never deep enough: it is a river mouth.
It will never bustle like New Plymouth.

Still, now and then, the flim-flam men turn up.
Wake up Council, and Ratepayers, wake up!

You are trying to revive a fossilised plesiosaur
by tending to its bones with caviar.

And don't start mouthing off about ironsand
and all its millions. The seabed will be ruined,

and any venture mothballed anyhow.
Just look at Waipipi—what is it now?

We'll have decimated fish stocks once they're gone,
and an injured ecosystem to pass on.

Cyrena

Entering port, she stranded on a shoal.
A log had stuck there, by an act of God,
and mud had banked up, after a heavy flood.
Her cargo: forty thousand cases of oil
brought from the East. That big log ripped her hull;
by midnight she was leaking something bad.
They beached her to the north, and thought they could
still float her off. She smashed up in a gale.

And lay there five months, till they blew her up
with such a charge that peoples' windows burst
and sitting hens went off their eggs. This here's
a case of silver spoons I bought, same type
as on my ship, but with her name. The last
ones left that weren't pinched. They're my souvenirs.

Control

Our airport gets a tower. Long live the modern!
I park the car, and stroll around its base.
I love to stand out here and think, my God, in
forty years or so we'll live in space.
I've loved the smell of aeroplane exhaust,
the roar of engines, all my life. The first
plane that I saw ripped through my ears, and coursed
its hydrocarbons through my blood. I'm cursed
to worship kerosene, wherever it burns.
But now, that tower . . . The problem is the sky.
So wide and pale whoever sees it learns
how small he is, how nothing we might fly
could scratch its skin. The tower, on its own,
so dwarfed, out here you only feel alone.

Walking the dog

You know those bunkers, built in World War Two
to guard the town from Japanese attacks,
as if they'd want to take this place . . . The tracks
along the river go past there, where you
might see teenagers huffing paint and glue,
but maybe you'll see something else that packs
more of a punch. We take it to the max,
and if you like to watch, I dare you to.

That's where I'll be tonight with my big girl—
I should say woman—ordering me round.
She comes down hard on me! And there'll be men
in other cars. Come on, give it a whirl;
whatever floats your boat might just be found.
We go there every Sunday night, round ten.

The long wait II

Hau always had to see his vengeance done.
I knew that he'd be wild when I went south
with two men, named for birds. Mouth after mouth
we spanned the rivers, till we came to one
I knew from stories, fast and full, too deep,
too wide to cross. A thousand sparkling eyes
of fish flashed in and out its jaws, the cries
of birds were woven into mine. Come sleep,
said Kiwi, wait until it calms—we'll swim
across it then. You're mad, I said, he'll come
for me and kill us all. And lying prone
upon the sand I listened. Ssh, it's him!
His voice was in the waves, their heavy thrum.
Somewhere he'd find me, turn me into stone.

South Beach Café

It used to be like going back in time
flying from here. In sixties dress, I wait;
the lounge unfortunately up-to-date,
sterile and bland. No orange plush, no grime,
no garish carpet squares that seem to chime
a discord with the walls. The tower's fate
sealed up with plywood boards. Proceed to gate.
I'll meet you for a drink. I'll make this rhyme.

But this, too, is the past: the winter light,
the lift-off over dunes, the bumpy ride,
the turbulence so wild I nearly spewed.
Time-travel is the only way I might
get back to you, the wine we drank outside.
And if that's not an option, then we're screwed.

Grace Dent

I struck, breached to, became a total wreck.
My bulky cargo quickly made me break,
the lightest piece a ton. My shattered deck,
my splintered masts, spoke to the clear mistake
my captain made, not mindful of the shore,
the pilot station's flags. He asked to cross,
they signalled *How much water do you draw?*
but no reply. The south wind put a gloss
of salt over his glass; the letters blurred.
Pounded on the sand, out came a spill
of ironbark; the timber sent to gird
the railway bridges. Read this how you will:
to cross the Tasman Sea in heavy gale
and reach the destination. Then to fail.

Pour

Like a twisted tap
like a sinking ship

like a cask of plonk
like a weeping drunk

like a turning tide
like a severed head

like a fatted cow
like those who know

like a steamer stack
like a sudden break

like an afterbirth
like the restless earth

let it all pour out.
Let it all pour out.

North Mole

We see Kupe climb out of his car
at the North Mole, pull his wetsuit
hood over his head, place foot after foot
on the sharp rocks towards where we are.
Hey man, he says, as he reaches the sand.
He's given up on the gym—
it doesn't motivate him.
He has more of a surfer's mind. And the band?
Yeah, yeah, his music is going well.
He times his movements to the swell;
so many things could lie beyond the roll
of water, out past the end of the mole.
And each wave curling in to the shore
is like the sea saying *what are you waiting for?*

Selected Bibliography

Anderson, Ken. *Sparse Timber Sawmillers: Ellis and Burnand Ltd., Sawmillers and Timber Merchants, Ongarue.* Taumarunui: Taumarunui and Districts Historical Society, 2008.

Binney, Judith. *Redemption Songs: A life of Te Kooti Arikirangi Te Turuki.* Wellington: Bridget Williams Books, 1995.

Burgess, J.S. 'Coastline change at Wanganui, New Zealand'. Diss. University of Canterbury, 1971.

Cooke, Ron. *Roll Back the Years: The Pictorial Magazine That Builds Up the History of Taumarunui and Surrounding District.* 7 vols. Taumarunui: C&S Publications, 1980–87.

Couper, Wilf, and Ron Cooke. *Kaitieke: The District, the People, the Schools.* 2nd ed. Taumarunui: C&S Publications, 1994.

Fleming, C.A. *The Geology of Wanganui Subdivision: Waverly and Wanganui Sheet Districts.* Wellington: Dept. of Scientific and Industrial Research, 1953.

Horizons Regional Council. *Whanganui Catchment Strategy: Updated Action Plan September 2003.* Palmerston North: Horizons Regional Council, 2003.

Kerry-Nicholls, J.H. *The King Country; Or, Explorations in New Zealand: A Narrative of 600 Miles of Travel Through Maoriland.* Christchurch: Capper Press, 1974.

Lowe, David, ed. *The Kakahi Sawmills.* Auckland: The Lodestar Press, 1978.

McMillan, Lyndsay, and Audrey Walker. *Ongarue: A Place of the Heart.* Ōngarue: Ongarue School Centenary Committee, 2005.

Mead, A.D. *Richard Taylor: Missionary Tramper.* Wellington: Reed, 1966.

Munro, Jessie, ed. *Letters on the Go: The Correspondence of Suzanne Aubert.* Wellington: Bridget Williams Books, 2009.

—. *The Story of Suzanne Aubert*. Auckland: Auckland University Press/Bridget Williams Books, 1996.

New Zealand Railway and Locomotive Society, Auckland Branch. *Ongarue Bush Tramway*. Auckland: New Zealand Railway and Locomotive Society, 1955.

New Zealand. Waitangi Tribunal. *Wai 167: The Whanganui River Report*. Wellington: Legislation Direct, 1999.

—. 'Wai 1130 Te Kāhui Maunga: The National Park District Inquiry Report'. *Ministry of Justice*. Ministry of Justice, n.d.

Parnell, Jim. *In the Wake of the Riverboats: Tales Told by Whanganui Riverboat Pioneers Joshua Harris and His Sons*. Wellington: Jim Parnell, 2005.

Reed, A.W. *Place Names of New Zealand*. Wellington: Reed, 1975.

Reid, Alec, and David Reid. *Paddle Wheels on the Wanganui*. Auckland: Blackwood and Janet Paul, 1967.

Smart, M.J.G., and A.P. Bates. *The Wanganui Story*. Whanganui: Wanganui Newspapers Ltd., 1972.

Walker, Audrey, and Ron Cooke. *Waimiha: People of Character*. Waimiha: Waimiha Reunion 2001 Committee, 2003.

Young, David. *Woven by Water: Histories from the Whanganui River*. Wellington: Huia, 1999.

The Whanganui Regional Museum, the online encyclopedia *Te Ara*, the National Library's *PapersPast* website, New Zealand History Online, and the New Zealand Electronic Text Collection have also been important sources of information.

This collection of poetry began life as the creative component of a PhD thesis in creative writing. For the full thesis see Beautrais, Airini. 'Narrativity and Segmentivity in Contemporary Australian and New Zealand Long Poems and Poem Sequences.' Diss. Victoria University of Wellington, 2016.

Acknowledgements

Many thanks are due to my two PhD supervisors, Harry Ricketts and James Brown, who have spent untold hours reading drafts of these poems and providing valuable feedback. Their dedicated and collegial approach has been much appreciated.

During 2013–16 I was fortunate to be part of a talented and supportive cohort of fellow PhD students at the International Institute of Modern Letters. Thanks to everyone for their friendship and feedback. I also thank Damien Wilkins and the other staff of the IIML, and my thesis examiners whose reports helped me refine a final draft.

Fergus Barrowman, Ashleigh Young and the team at Victoria University Press have given me guidance, strength and support in turning a manuscript into a book. They've been as wonderful to work with as ever.

Some of these poems have been previously published in print and online journals and zines. Thanks are due to the editors of *Landfall*, *Overland*, *Blackmail Press*, *Food Court*, *Sport*, *IKA*, *SWAMP*, *Turbine* and *Best New Zealand Poems*.

I would like to thank the people who have provided me with verbal information and stories relating to the Whanganui catchment, river and town: Stephen King, Nelson Lebo, Lieze Thomson, Michael Goessi, and my parents Margie and Keith Beautrais.

Josef Beautrais provided generous assistance with the making of maps. Data from LINZ was used, along with imagery from Geographx.

Finally, I acknowledge the many poets, both contemporary and historical, anonymous and canonical, whose forms I have pillaged and whose lines I've alluded to.